The Naked Voice

The
Naked
Voice

A Wholistic Approach to Singing

W. STEPHEN SMITH

with MICHAEL CHIPMAN

OXFORD
UNIVERSITY PRESS

2007

OXFORD

UNIVERSITY PRESS

Oxford University Press, Inc., publishes works that further
Oxford University's objective of excellence
in research, scholarship, and education.

Oxford   New York
Auckland   Cape Town   Dar es Salaam   Hong Kong   Karachi
Kuala Lumpur   Madrid   Melbourne   Mexico City   Nairobi
New Delhi   Shanghai   Taipei   Toronto

With offices in
Argentina   Austria   Brazil   Chile   Czech Republic   France   Greece
Guatemala   Hungary   Italy   Japan   Poland   Portugal   Singapore
South Korea   Switzerland   Thailand   Turkey   Ukraine   Vietnam

Published by Oxford University Press, Inc.
198 Madison Avenue, New York, New York 10016

www.oup.com

Oxford is a registered trademark of Oxford University Press

Library of Congress Cataloging-in-Publication Data
Smith, W. Stephen.
The naked voice : a wholistic approach to singing /
W. Stephen Smith with Michael Chipman.
p. cm.
Includes index.
ISBN 978-0-19-530050-5
1. Singing—Instruction and study. 2. Voice culture.
I. Chipman, Michael. II. Title.
MT820.S697 2007
783'.043—dc22   2006017220

19 18 17 16 15 14

Printed in the United States of America
on acid-free paper

This book is dedicated to my students.

— W. STEPHEN SMITH

The Prologue to Pagliacci
by Leoncavallo

Translation by W. Stephen Smith

If you please? Ladies! Gentlemen! Excuse me if alone I present myself.
  I am the Prologue.

Once again the author wishes to put the old characters on the stage.
  In part he wants to return to the old usage,
  but he sends to you a new messenger—me.

But not to tell you as before:
  "The tears that we shed are false!
  Don't be alarmed by our sufferings and torments."
  No! No!

Instead the author has sought to paint for you a slice of life.
  He has for his maxim only that the artist is a man,
  and that for men he must write.
  Truth was his inspiration!

A nest of memories sang in the depth of his soul one day,
  and with real tears he wrote while his sobs beat time for him!
  Therefore, you will see love just as human beings love.
  You will see the wretched fruits of hatred and the spasms of sadness,
  You will hear howls of rage and cynical laughter!

And you, rather than just looking at our outward garb,
consider our souls.
  Because we are men of flesh and bone,
  and just like you,
  we breathe the same air of this orphaned world!

The concept I have told you.
  Now listen how it is unfolded.
  Let's go! Begin!

Acknowledgments

This book would not exist without the help and support of many people. Jeffrey T. Hopper provided an inspirational voice and crucial perspective at the conceptual stage and constant encouragement and suggestions throughout the writing process. Edith Bers and Vinson Cole read early versions of the proposal and gave generous support to the idea. Eva Archer-Smith shared her expertise as an executive and life coach to help us solidify the scope and reach of the book. Special thanks go to JaNel VanDenBerghe for her meticulous proofreading and fresh eye in preparing the final proposal.

Claudia Friedlander's knowledge of human anatomy helped when compiling images for the art manuscript, and David Fry's technological genius made the writing and editing process not only bearable but enjoyable.

Many thanks to current and former students who contributed feedback for the manuscript, including Ferris Allen, Sara Allison, Christine Armistead, Laura Avery, Holly Bewlay, Karen Boychuk, Christine Brewer, Ken Bryson, Robert Chionis, Sasha Cooke, Alice Conway, Joe Davisson, Phyllis Demetropoulos, Mazias De Oliveira, Tanya Deiter, Joyce DiDonato, Gretchen Farrar, Claudia Friedlander, Brian Frutiger, Waldo Gonzalez, James Heffel, Catherine Heraty, Christopher Herbert, Teri Herron, Weston Hurt, Tiffany Jackson, Bangsool Kim, Sunyoung Kim, Jonathan Knapp, Nicole Heaston Lane, Ricardo Lugo,

VaShawn McIlwain, Tobey D. Miller, Andrew Milligan, Jeff Monette, Jennifer Moore Poretta, Matthew Morris, Scott Murphree, Marti Newland, Gale Oxley, Tina Parker, Alex Huzhuang Qian, Evan Rogister, Heidi Moss Sali, Rolando Sanz, Aric Schneller, Michael Slattery, Michael Smallwood, Annette Sondock, Deborah Stinson, Susan Stone Taborn, Jonathan Taylor, Emily Tepe, Laca Tines, Kimako Trotman, Leah Tsamous, Josh Winograde, and Chenye Yuan.

We are also grateful to the singers who generously donated their time and talents to provide audio samples on the CD accompanying this book. They include Aaron Blake, Amy Buckley, Christina Carr, Ross Chitwood, Sasha Cooke, Joyce DiDonato, Claudia Friedlander, David Salsbery Fry, Weston Hurt, Julie Liston Johnson, Tobey D. Miller, Brian Mulligan, Scott Murphree, Anne Jennifer Nash, Marti Newland, Gene Roberts, Evan Rogister, Kathryn Skemp, Stephanie E. Tennill, and Jennifer Zetlan. Also thanks to Bob Taibbi, the recording engineer at Juilliard, for his expert help in creating the audio sample CD.

Kay Gowen, Emily Jobe, Carolyn Ososfsky, Abby Smith, and Suanne Walker gave generously of their time and intellect to proofread both the initial proposal and final manuscript. They provided feedback and corrections, which clarified and simplified the book. A special thanks goes to Gene Roberts who enthusiastically read the manuscript and then helped proof the art work and final copies.

Finally, Carol Smith was an anchor of quiet encouragement from the earliest conceptual stages through the final edits. In addition to creating the title of the book, Carol provided constant and insightful help (not to mention delicious meals) during the editing process, often finding the perfect phrase or word when we were stumped. She also contributed her significant skill as a pianist and computer wizard to create the musical examples in Finale. This book would not exist without her steadfast support.

Preface

I have been privileged to play a significant role in the publication of this book. Having studied voice with Steve Smith for five years, I found his approach to singing to be elegant, powerful, and totally unique. I felt that a book about his techniques and philosophies would be an important addition to the existing literature on singing and vocal pedagogy (not to mention my own bookshelf).

Over the years, many people had suggested to Steve that he should write a book, but I proposed to him that with my background as a professional writer, singer, and voice student, I might be the one to help him get it done. He agreed, and we started moving forward with the process. That process entailed writing a proposal, finding a publisher, then recording dozens of hours of interviews with Steve, each one focused on a specific topic for the various chapters of the book. Over the course of a year, I transcribed those interviews word for word, edited them into readable prose, and then Steve, his wife, Carol, and I combed through each chapter in great detail many times, making sure every sentence accurately and authentically reflected his ideas.

I emphasize that I take no credit whatsoever for any of the ideas, opinions, philosophies, or techniques laid out in this book. My only intent from the very beginning has been to communicate Steve's ideas in his voice and in his words with clarity and simplicity.

Although this book cannot take the place of regular private lessons, I hope it will be a powerful supplemental tool for singers and singing teachers. Readers should know that every sentence of every chapter was painstakingly crafted to present an accurate reflection of Steve's remarkable approach to singing. Based on personal experience, I believe that anyone interested in singing better will benefit from careful study of the philosophies and techniques included herein.

For over a decade I have been on an amazing journey as a writer and singer. I could not have undertaken this journey alone, and I offer profound thanks to my former voice teachers Tricia Swanson, Marla Volovna, Jean Ronald LaFond, and especially Betty Jeanne Chipman and Richard Miller. I owe a special debt of gratitude to Steve Smith, whose patience and encouragement put me on the path to discovering my true voice. I must also thank my mentors at Utah State University, Joyce Kinkead and Brian McCuskey, who taught me to write with focus and simplicity and to seek out the truth inherent in paradox. Finally, Jan Beatty at Oxford University Press has been a fine and gracious editor, and I am honored to have worked with her and Steve on this life-changing project.

MICHAEL CHIPMAN

Contents

The Naked Voice

Introduction

In Pursuit of Authenticity

I have spent my professional career teaching singers how to undress (vocally, emotionally, and psychologically). My goal is to help them clear away the entanglements, hang-ups, insecurities, habits, and fears that keep their voices from singing true and free. The process is sometimes long and difficult, but often rewarding and crucial to personal and professional success.

In my teaching, I try to communicate simply and directly. I have tried to do the same in this book. When I told one of my students about this project, he said that it should have "as much Arkansas in it as possible" (I was born and raised in Arkansas). With that in mind, I have attempted to make the style of writing straightforward and accessible.

This book is intended for all who desire to sing or improve their singing. The concepts are designed to help singers—from the amateur in the local church choir to the world-famous opera star—strip away the encumbrances that keep them from revealing their essential, "naked voice." In the process they uncover their truest, most authentic selves.

The word *naked* usually refers to the physical body, and for me conjures images of Adam and Eve blissfully nude in the Garden of Eden. They didn't know they were naked, so they were not ashamed. Eating the forbidden fruit made them aware of good and evil and filled them with shame, so they began the process of covering up. We evidently are in a similar state of shame because we are still covering our nakedness—hence, the emergence of the multibillion-dollar fashion industry, which is devoted to this idea.

The way in which we cover ourselves and the amount of skin we cover says a lot about who and what we are, and in our culture those cover-ups (i.e., our clothes) often define our differences. In corporate America, "clothes make the man," and job applicants are told that the cardinal rule of job interviews is to "dress for success." How we dress tells how we want to be perceived.

Nakedness levels the playing field and connotes something essential, pure, unfettered, and authentic. Nakedness also refers to the process of stripping off our metaphorical clothes to reveal our essence—our uniqueness and individuality. This kind of honesty is especially important in the performing arts, where the audience seeks an immediate connection with the performers on stage. Although they might not understand this exchange on a conscious level, I think the audience senses when performers give an honest performance. They also sense when they don't.

Why do we go to the theater or the opera? I believe that deep down, every person wants to be authentic, and great performers help us connect with that part of ourselves. Achieving authenticity is not an easy process, especially when most societal organizations and institutions need us to conform to a certain set of rules, to fit a particular mode, to "cover up" in a certain way. I am not a nonconformist; on the contrary, I understand that in conforming or relating to social pressures we come to understand our identity and place in the world. However, the process of returning to our essence—our most basic self—requires us to strip away our cover-ups and reexamine society's rules and conventions to discover truths that might have been obscured over time.

Through this process of stripping away, we grow up. We question the values, rules, and expectations that have been given to us, and we reject them, modify them, or embrace them as our own. That ownership is the key to releasing our fears and insecurities, accepting our gifts and abilities, and rediscovering the original passions that were given to us at birth. Having rediscovered that essential nature, we can endeavor to act with integrity in every aspect of life. No one does that perfectly or completely; the value is in the *pursuit*.

I have been pursuing authenticity for much of my life. I confess to falling short of that goal; but experience has taught me that authenticity is a process, not a destination. Deep in everyone's soul is a longing for authenticity. However, because the journey is long and hard and requires a constant rejection of the status quo, many don't even begin. Others quit when fear and insecurity set in.

The Naked Voice: A Wholistic Approach to Singing is a book about how to sing, but it is also about the pursuit of authenticity. Singing is the metaphor for that pursuit, and here it is much more—singing provides an immediate physical application of my ideas and philosophies in a practical way. Many of my students have found that the process of learning to sing is intricately connected to their personal development. Although my philosophies and techniques are focused on good singing, my students often become more authentic people along the way. Their moments of discovery are my greatest joy in teaching, and I am humbled to be part of that process. I have gratefully woven many of their stories into the narrative of this book.

My philosophies and techniques are inseparable from my personal history, so I will share some of my story to highlight the pivotal moments in my journey. In these moments, I made choices that defied the expectations of my family, church, and society. I am not telling this as a model for anyone else to follow; it is simply *my* story and a way to "expose myself" and my unique path. I respect each person's path and am intrigued by every story. Just as no two voices are the same, every path is unique.

My Story

I was born in a small town in northeast Arkansas in 1950, the fifth of five children, to parents who grew up poor during the Depression. Because my dad was the second of eleven children and my mom the second of nine, they were both taught that working hard and caring for your family were the only essentials in life. My mom never held a paying job after my parents were married, because women were supposed to "stay home, have babies, and fry meat."

We were members of the Church of Christ, a conservative fundamentalist religion in which singing was very important. My dad's father taught shape-note singing during "gospel meetings." All singing was a cappella (without instrumental accompaniment) and people were expected to learn to sing in four-part harmony. Everyone in my family could sing parts, and we often sang together in church or just for fun.

During my third-grade year we got a piano, which Dad had accepted as barter payment for a car at his Ford dealership. Two of my sisters began piano lessons but stopped after two months when their teacher quit because of her pregnancy. When I was in sixth grade, I heard a friend play a piano piece in a minor key that resonated deeply with me, and I wanted to learn to play it. My dad was opposed to the idea of a boy, especially *his* son, taking piano lessons and refused to pay for them. So that summer, I mowed a neighbor's lawn for

$1.25 each week to pay for my own lessons. This was the first of several choices that defied conventional expectations. After the summer was over, my mom paid for the lessons. At the end of one year of study, my piano teacher moved away, so I stopped taking lessons but continued to play on my own.

When it came time to go to college, I didn't know which career path to pursue. My skills and interests were broad—I was good in math and considered a career in medicine—but in my heart I wanted to study music. Following in the path of my siblings before me, I enrolled at Harding College. Although I had very little formal musical training, I began as a music major because I played clarinet and piano as well as anyone in my little town. I didn't consider voice my primary instrument because all my siblings sang, and I did not think my singing talent was special.

At the end of my first year, Dad threatened to cut off my funding if I didn't change my major to something more practical. A fierce argument ensued after which I decided to major in both music and math. Calculus homework, however, was incredibly time-consuming and detracted from my music practice, so I dropped the math major halfway through the year. Choosing to major exclusively in music was another pivotal moment for me, challenging cultural norms and my dad's threats to follow my heart.

Parallel to my pursuit of music, I also began a quest for a more authentic faith. I had always been a "good little boy," obeying all the rules without argument or question. In the summer after my freshman year, I toured Europe for ten weeks with my college chorus. That experience opened my eyes and my mind to a whole new world, particularly when a chorus alumna challenged me to read the Bible to see what it truly said and not just to find evidence in it to prove my religion was correct.

During the next year I began to read the Bible simply to see what it said— something I had never done before. Through that pursuit of truth I came to the ultimate question: Did I believe in the existence of God? Because His existence couldn't be proven, I decided to live existentially—to indulge any passion, feeling, desire, or compulsion without regard for reward or punishment. The next twenty-four hours were the most painful and tormented of my life.

Emerging from that test of faith, I began to reconstruct my beliefs, not according to the teachings of my church or culture but according to what I believed deep down to be true, based on what I read in the Bible. In effect, I created a religion of my own, which externally didn't look very different from the one in which I was raised, but internally was totally new. I developed a set of beliefs for which I took full responsibility. That process continues for me to this day.

It seems that I was programmed for this pursuit of authenticity: evaluating the information provided by society, education, family, church, and my community, sifting through it, throwing out portions, and creating something that seemed true to me. It was this same process by which I developed techniques for teaching singing.

I married Carol Mannen, a great musician and pianist in her own right, during our senior year of college. We agreed that because we were musicians, we would probably never be wealthy. My career goal was to teach college music classes—theory, conducting, and singing were all interesting to me. I decided to pursue graduate work in voice because that degree program appeared more interesting than theory or conducting. Out of naiveté and lack of proper counsel, I applied *only* to Indiana University and was not accepted. So we made plans to move back to my hometown and work for my dad with an eye to eventually taking over his business. Recognizing my musical and singing talents, my college piano teacher and her singer/doctor husband (Neva and Bill White) intervened and convinced us that this move might be a big mistake. Bill took me to his alma mater (the University of Arkansas) and introduced me to his former teacher, Richard Brothers, under whom I earned my master's degree.

I never really intended to pursue a career in performing, but I realized that to get a college teaching position, I needed performing experience. That practical need was my main impetus for pursuing a performing career. However, the same year I earned my master's degree, I was hired as a one-year replacement for the choir director at Oklahoma Christian College. While there, Carol and I did a lot of performing for college development functions, banquets and so forth, and the college administration appreciated us so much that they created a faculty position to keep me there. Besides teaching voice lessons, I produced and directed musicals and operas, taught music theory, sight-singing, keyboard harmony, ear training, and all the vocal music education classes. I stayed there eleven years.

During my first year in Oklahoma, I became interested in the work of a famous voice teacher, the late Inez Lunsford Silberg, who taught at Oklahoma City University. Several of her current and former students were building successful international opera careers at the time, and I was curious about her teaching style and technique. I began studying with Mrs. Silberg and with her encouragement, I enrolled at OCU for a second master's degree in opera performance. She used abstract imagery almost exclusively to convey the kind of sound she wanted me to produce, and I was able to intuit what I needed to do physically and mentally to make the sound happen. She and I developed a strong connection because I was able to apply the ideas she gave me. I credit her with teaching me what a great sound should be.

While I was studying with Mrs. Silberg, several of the singers in her studio seemed frustrated because they didn't understand her imagery and abstract concepts. So after a performance class where singers seemed to be confused, I would approach them and explain in more practical, physical terms what I thought she meant. In that way, I began to help my colleagues move forward in their technical progress. Although I honor Mrs. Silberg for what she taught me, I developed my own teaching style and vocal technique, which were very different from those I learned from any other teacher.

I won some competitions, and at the age of thirty-two I had an apprenticeship at Des Moines Metro Opera. That summer I realized I probably could have an operatic singing career, but I wasn't as compelled to sing as the other apprentices were. I decided that the world would be no worse off if I didn't have a singing career, but it might be worse off if I didn't teach. I also had two young daughters and a wife I wanted to support, and the lifestyle of the itinerant singer was not appealing. Furthermore, I didn't need to pursue a performing career to get a college teaching job—I already had one. After that summer I never again pursued a career in performance, even though I have continued to perform in the occasional opera, concert, or recital. In contrast to many singing teachers who have had successful performing careers, I consciously and willingly chose to devote my career to teaching rather than to performing.

I taught voice lessons and performed at Inspiration Point Fine Arts Colony (now called Opera in the Ozarks) in the summer of 1985. At that time, it became clear to me that training people for professional careers in opera and musicals was my passion. In pursuing this more focused teaching field, I was hired as chair of the Voice Department at the St. Louis Conservatory, which closed after my third year there. I then took a job at the University of Houston, where I also taught voice for the Houston Grand Opera Studio. My work there led to a position at the Aspen Music Festival and School, and the Aspen connection led to my current position at Juilliard. Along the way, I gradually developed an approach for teaching singing that was unique to me. In each position, I attempted to do my best and be true to myself.

The current flowing through my story has been a pursuit of authenticity. The story is not a model for anyone else to follow—it is simply *my* story. My goal in teaching voice is to help people write their own authentic stories—to find their voices and themselves, not by pretending to be something different than what they are but by being themselves—fully, truly, and openly.

And the pursuit is not over.

My students are the motivation for this book. Over the years, many of them have asked me to write down my ideas and techniques in a book, but I have been reluctant to do so. I thought I didn't have the time to write, and I felt that none of my ideas was particularly original. The originality comes from the way I organize and communicate those ideas. The value in this book is not in the information it contains but in its application.

Another reason I decided to write this book is that even though I only teach people to sing, many students have told me that the process of learning to sing has dramatically changed their lives. It has been a common but miraculous experience to see this happen over and over again. I love to teach people to sing, but it is especially gratifying to know that I am giving people tools that might help them live more fulfilled and happy lives.

The book is divided into three parts. Part I (Basic Instincts) presents the philosophies, principles, and ideas behind what I teach. The techniques don't make much sense out of the context of the principles on which they are based. Much of the lesson time is devoted to the practical, physical application of exercises. However, I begin my work with every student who enters my studio by giving what I call "the spiel." This is a basic overview of my philosophies and a brief explanation of how those philosophies apply to singing. I have followed the same format here, introducing the philosophy and then the technique.

Part II (The Inventions) explains how I have distilled the philosophies and principles down into six exercises, which I call "Inventions." As with all of the chapter titles in this book, the term *invention* has multiple meanings. A mechanical invention involves taking existing materials and putting them together for a new and unique purpose. I have done this by gleaning the best information I came across on the function of the singing voice and creating exercises to apply that information in a practical way. The term also gives a nod to the musical inventions of J. S. Bach in which he took a musical idea and expanded upon it with new contrapuntal concepts. These Inventions are not especially brilliant or revolutionary, but the way I organize and apply them is unique. They emerged out of the need to convey the principles of free, authentic singing in a clear and simple procedure.

Part III (Where the Rubber Meets the Road) addresses how the skills gained in the six Inventions apply to everyday life as a singer. It includes chapters about applying the technique to repertoire and how one successfully navigates the treacherous waters of a singing career. The advice given in these chapters is firmly rooted in the original philosophy I introduce in Part I.

I hope this book provides a fresh perspective on singing. This approach is not *definitive* but *different* from others. It is different only because it is my own assimilation of concepts I have found helpful to singers. I have intended to make the ideas accessible to anyone who is interested in singing at any level. Revealing the naked voice is a constant challenge for all singers—from that soprano in the local church choir to the world-famous diva—and the principles in this book apply to singers at any point in that process. People who discover their naked voice and maintain a sense of authenticity have longer and more fulfilling careers than those who look at singing solely as a means to material success.

Finally, our voices are an expression of the deepest reaches of our souls. In writing this book, I hope to help people find their naked voice so that every word they sing has a pure, complete sound, expressed straight from the heart. It is a complex, multilevel process, but throughout my career and in writing this book, I have distilled the concepts down to their essence. Singing is a magical, miraculous thing. I don't pretend to work miracles or magic when I teach. I only help people free their voice so that the miracles happen on their own—all the time.

Part

I

BASIC INSTINCTS

A Wholistic Approach to Singing

Wholism is a philosophy that considers all the various aspects of the human experience—physical, mental, emotional, spiritual, and so forth. I will explain how my approach to singing falls into a *wholistic* category later in this chapter. First, I would like to discuss the title of Part I of this book: Basic Instincts.

What are our most basic instincts? When we strip away all our complicated layers of cultural conditioning and neurosis, what is left? Our most basic instincts are the first two things we do in life: breathing and speaking. Breathing is the first life-giving activity after birth. Before making any sound, we breathe. Speaking is the first creative activity after birth. (We actually begin with phonation—the vibration of the vocal cords—which later evolves into speech.) When we come out wailing, we affirm that we are alive, and that wailing itself is a creative activity—the pure expression of fear or discomfort in our new surroundings. Those two foundational elements enable us to express ourselves throughout life.

We express ourselves by making sounds—through speaking, and, for those reading this book, through singing. As a foundation for the exercises and ideas to come, it is important to understand the basic ingredients of how we make sound—specifically, musical sound.

Making a musical sound requires three ingredients: a *generator*, a *vibrator*, and a *resonator*. This fact of acoustics can be found in almost any physics textbook. The generator is something that moves. That movement causes the vibrator to vibrate. The resonator is something in the vicinity of the vibrator that vibrates sympathetically with it, and thus amplifies and helps define the quality of the sound.

For example, when I play the piano, the generator is my finger mashing the key. When I mash the key, the action of the piano causes the hammer to strike a string (the vibrator). My finger pressing the key is an indirect action that vibrates the string. The piano's sounding board, placed next to the vibrator, is the primary resonator. Piano builders carefully design the sounding board using different types of porous wood that are glued together to achieve premium color and quality in the sound. The sounding board gives the piano a big, full sound and helps define the timbre (or quality) of the sound—this is why a piano doesn't sound like a banjo.

In a guitar, the generator is the finger plucking the string. That action vibrates the string (the vibrator), and the body of the guitar is the primary resonator for the sound. In stringed instruments, including the violin, viola, cello, and bass, the musician's bow arm is the generator. As the bow is pulled across the string, the string vibrates, and, like the guitar, the body of the violin is the resonator.

In woodwind instruments, such as the clarinet, oboe, English horn, and bassoon, airflow is the generator. The air moves across a reed (the vibrator), which vibrates and makes a sound. The instrument itself is the resonator for the sound.

In brass instruments, airflow is also the generator, the lips are the vibrators and the instrument itself is the resonator. As with the piano, the shape and type of the resonator for a brass instrument makes a big difference in the quality of the sound. A trumpet made of wood instead of brass would not sound like a trumpet. Wood vibrates and mellows the sound, whereas the conical shape and metal of a brass instrument primarily projects the fundamental tone.

Finally, we come to the human voice. Speaking in purely acoustical terms, airflow is the generator, the vocal folds (which are located inside the larynx or voice box, behind the Adam's apple—see figure 1.1) are the vibrators, and the primary resonators are the nasal cavity, mouth, and pharynx. (The vocal folds are commonly referred to as *cords*. I will occasionally use those terms interchangeably in this book.) The physical function of the voice is most akin to someone playing a brass instrument, and the comparison between the two is useful in understanding how the voice works.

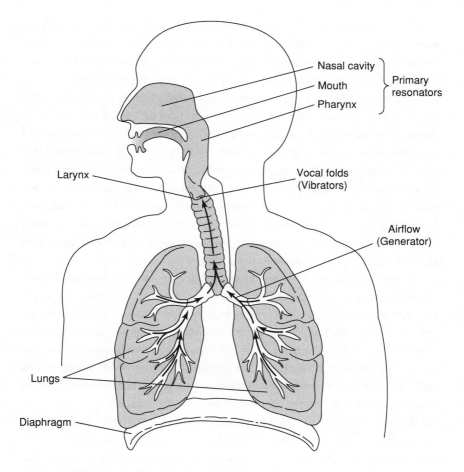

FIGURE 1.1. Mechanism for producing the human voice

As with a trumpet or trombone, singers need airflow to make sounds, and the vibration of the vocal folds is very similar to the vibration of brass players' lips. For brass players to play low notes, they relax their lips to be short and thick, and the full length of both lips vibrates. For high notes they stretch their lips long and thin, and a smaller portion of the lips vibrates.

A similar thing happens with vocal folds. When we sing low notes, the folds relax to become thicker and shorter, and the full length of the folds vibrates; for higher notes, the folds stretch longer and thinner, and a smaller portion of the folds vibrates. The difference is that brass players' lips stretch longer from both ends (as when smiling), whereas the vocal folds are attached in the front of the larynx and stretch mostly backward. The similarity is in the way a brass player's lips buzz and the way the vocal folds buzz.

As a brass player buzzes his or her lips, puffs of air are emitted from the mouth. These puffs of air make waves in the air that hit the eardrum. Similarly, vibrating vocal folds emit puffs of air in a regular pattern. The brass player's lips also flop in and out, similar to the vocal folds undulating up and down.

This type of buzzing of the vocal folds is called *phonation*. When we phonate, the folds are adducted (or pulled together) so that as air flows through them waves are emitted. As air comes up underneath the folds, they start to separate under the pressure. As they open, a puff of air passes through, and that puff of air then sucks the cords back together. This suction is known in physics as the *Bernoulli effect* (see figure 1.2). The Bernoulli effect occurs when two objects are pulled together by air passing between them. However, during phonation there is not a constant abduction and adduction (opening and closing) of the folds. They are always adducted, but the air flowing through causes them to touch and separate many times per second.

The entire body is a resonator because all the tissue of the body will vibrate sympathetically to some degree with the vibration in the vocal folds. However, the *primary* resonators are the cavities through which the air flows after buzzing the vocal folds. The air flows from the lungs through the bronchial tubes and into the trachea, where it unites with the vocal folds. The primary resonators are the area above that: the mouth, the pharynx (the area behind the mouth and above the throat), and the nasal cavities (the spaces behind and above the nose, which used to be shown in sinus medicine commercials—see figure 1.1). All those cavities are connected by air passages. The vibration in these resonators is what increases amplitude and quality in our sound.

Although the chest cavity also resonates, it is a secondary resonator. We feel vibration in the chest because it is a large cavity near the vocal folds, and it vibrates sympathetically. However, the major impact on amplitude and quality comes after the air has passed through the larynx, so the mouth and pharynx are the primary resonators. The shape of the mouth and the pharynx constantly change as we articulate words (i.e., vowels and consonants). We cannot voluntarily change the shape of the nasal cavities (even though they can change their shape with sinus congestion). So resonance is always changing as we change the size and shape of the mouth and pharynx.

Because we can change the shape and size of our primary resonators, it might seem as though we could manufacture resonance. However, resonance is always passive. It is a response to another vibration—it is something that just happens, not something we do. We seem to be able to make resonance happen in a specific place and are therefore lulled into thinking that it is active rather than passive. This concept is often referred to as *placement*, meaning we are

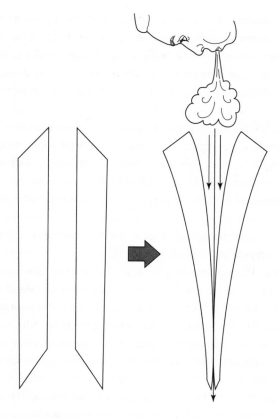

FIGURE 1.2. The Bernoulli effect

putting resonance in a specific place. However, the nature of resonance is passive response and can't really be placed anywhere.

Once we understand that resonance is *passive*, we must focus our attention on the two *active* ingredients in singing: phonation and airflow. With those concepts in hand, singing can become simple: We learn how to phonate efficiently and train our air to flow freely.

THE SINGER'S DILEMMA

Despite all the parallels I just described, the voice is not a trumpet or trombone. All musical instruments other than the voice are mechanical objects, and the goal in playing them is to manipulate the object efficiently. The voice, however, is not mechanical, and since its three components (generator, vibrator, and resonator) are located inside our bodies, we cannot directly observe or manipulate them. Additionally, their function is subject to human nature, and human nature is a complex mix of intellectual, spiritual, emotional, physical, and psychological aspects. All of these things are unobservable and nonmechanical, yet they have a direct impact on our ability to sing with efficiency and freedom. Therein lies the singer's dilemma.

Because a mechanical approach works for other instruments, it would seem logical to think of singing as mechanical. Indeed, many people approach singing as though the voice were a mechanical instrument: Just punch a button and you get a certain response. But the voice does not work that way. Singers certainly follow scientific principles (physiological and acoustical), but singing is not a mechanical process.

The scientific principles of singing are fascinating, but understanding them doesn't necessarily make people sing better. Some singers who know very little about the process sing beautifully; others know a lot about that process and sing poorly. I do not mean to disparage scientific research in singing—there has been much valuable research on the function of the voice and the acoustical properties of good singing—but scientific analysis can only tell us what *happens* when we sing. It cannot tell us what we must *do* to sing well. What *happens* when we sing well often has little to do with what we *do* in singing.

A scientific approach to singing misses the big picture. Although we can look at our vocal cords through a laryngoscope and chart the various formants of acoustical sound, we cannot chart the effects of body, mind, and heart on the voice—and those things are as much a part of the instrument as are the vocal folds themselves. Because our entire person is our instrument, everything about us—our physical, emotional, intellectual, psychological, and spiritual state of being—affects the physical and acoustical aspects of singing.

THE WHOLISTIC APPROACH

What, then, is the solution to the singer's dilemma? We should take an approach to singing that deals with our whole selves, that takes our multifaceted nature into account—the intellectual, spiritual, psychological, emotional, physical, and acoustical aspects of the human experience. As I mentioned earlier, it is not unusual for people to approach singing as a mechanical process, but "mechanical" is not a part of our nature. And while it is helpful to understand the physiological and acoustical aspects of singing, those aspects alone are limited in their scope. Good technique must deal with the whole human organism.

This is why I take a Wholistic Approach to Singing. I realize many readers might think I am spelling the word *wholistic* incorrectly. Wholism is often used as a synonym of *holism*, a term associated with Gestalt psychology. *Gestalt* is a German word meaning "shape" or "form" but is used in English to mean "an organized whole that is perceived as more than the sum of its parts" (*Oxford American Dictionary*). *Holism* refers only to the connection of body, mind, and spirit, whereas *wholism* encompasses all aspects of the human experience. I cannot fix the whole by fixing each of its parts. I start with the whole, and every part is examined in relationship to the whole.

I use a simple concept—one unified whole—that includes all the various aspects of human nature. This wholistic concept focuses on what we do to sing healthily and right rather than focusing on fixing what is wrong. It is what we do, not what we avoid. Although *holism* is included in *wholism*, I prefer the spelling that encompasses the bigger picture. To help understand my approach to singing, I contrast my experiences with a conventional doctor and a holistic doctor.

Conventional Medicine versus Holistic Medicine

Holistic medicine is gaining ground in conventional modern medical practice. I first encountered it when I visited a holistic doctor several years ago. The field of modern medicine seems to be concerned with finding antidotes to illnesses; when people get sick they take medicine, which eliminates the illness. Drugs and antibiotics have become extremely important tools because they ended plagues and eliminated the threat of illnesses that once seemed destined to wipe us out. Diseases like leprosy, polio, and smallpox have been all but obliterated because of drugs and antibiotics. The field of modern medicine emerged out of the period in which drugs were used to solve these terrible problems and cure seemingly incurable diseases. The medical field became focused on the power of chemicals (i.e., drugs) to solve problems. Drugs do serve a crucial, valuable purpose in eliminating these diseases or at least making them treatable.

When I go to a conventional doctor, my goal is to leave with a prescription. I present symptoms of my illness, and I want an antidote to eliminate those symptoms. The doctor diagnoses my illness and prescribes the right medicine. If the doctor has diagnosed correctly and I take the prescribed medicine, those symptoms will disappear. The conventional method works. However, the conventional doctor may not seem to be concerned with *why* I got sick—the pathology of my illness, or where it came from. Instead, his or her goal (and mine) is to eliminate my symptoms. If I have a chronic illness, I must keep taking the medicine for the symptoms to stay away. In this sense, all medicine is a temporary cure because it treats only the symptoms—not the source—of the illness.

With this approach, the unspoken assumption is that I was completely healthy before these symptoms appeared, so if I eliminate the symptoms with the right medicine, I will return to full health. That is not an accurate assumption, however, because I may have no symptoms of illness and still be unhealthy.

By contrast, when I went to a holistic doctor, he first put me on a diet to get the right nutrients feeding my body. He then suggested an exercise program to help regulate my metabolism. Then he recommended a meditation program to address the mental aspects of my health. If I got sick, he could give me a prescription, but he was concerned with *why* I got sick—whether I blew my diet, quit exercising, or stopped the meditation. The assumption of holistic medicine is that I will avoid most illness if I maintain my health through diet, exercise, and meditation. It is a preventive approach, and though it is not a panacea, it has made some profound changes in the medical profession. Most health care practitioners now emphasize the importance of health maintenance through proper diet and exercise. Medications are, of course, valuable and sometimes essential, but fewer people see them as the ultimate solution anymore.

The most common approach to teaching voice is similar to the conventional doctor's method. When a singer shows up with vocal problems (symptoms), the teacher offers "medicine" for each problem. The unspoken assumption, as with the conventional doctor, is that before the symptoms occurred the singer had no vocal production issues, so if the teacher eliminates the symptoms, all vocal problems will be solved. This makes no more sense than believing we are always perfectly healthy until we get sick. Even singers with no symptoms of unhealthy singing can improve the health of their singing process.

For example, if a singer always sings flat on a particular pitch, the teacher might say, "At that pitch you must always smile and lift your cheeks." That may fix the intonation problem on that pitch, but it won't solve the deeper problem of *why* the singer was flat on that note. "Smile and lift the cheeks" works like a prescription. I call it a "trick" because it is a temporary fix. These tricks or prescriptions do not address the problem at its source, but because they do temporarily make singing better (like taking medicine), the singer is lulled into thinking that this approach can solve any problem. However, if the problem is not addressed at its root, it will reappear as a different symptom at a later time, which will require another trick to fix it. The ultimate outcome of this approach is that the singer sounds like a bag of tricks and is still, underneath it all, unhealthy.

My approach to singing is similar to the holistic medicine approach. Only in the first hearing of a student do I focus on what is wrong (the symptoms). After that hearing, I focus on what singers need to *do* to develop and maintain free and healthy singing (just as the holistic doctor focuses on diet, health, and meditation) and not on the habits and tensions that must be eliminated. When I deal with a symptom of a vocal problem, I am concerned with finding the root cause of the symptom, much like the holistic doctor is concerned about the cause of my illness. I establish a hierarchy of correct (i.e., healthy) things to do, which will ultimately eliminate the problem, along with its symptoms.

So conventional medicine focuses on what is *wrong* with the patient, whereas holistic medicine focuses on what the patient needs to *do right*. We address both the positive and negative in wholistic singing, but the focus is on the positive. I am not so idealistic as to believe that we can deal only with the positive all the time, but maintaining a focus on the positive simplifies and clarifies the process. For example, if I tell someone to turn right at a particular intersection, I am also telling him not to turn left or go straight (those negative instructions are inherent). But isn't it much simpler just to say, "turn right" instead of "do not turn left or go straight?" Also, if I only say, "do not turn left or go straight," I am omitting the crucial positive instruction: "Turn right." Focusing on what singers need to *stop doing* does not necessarily let them know what they need to *do* that is right.

What, then, is that crucial positive focus in singing, the gestalt concept that will always keep a singer on the right track? It is speaking. *Speaking* is the original creative activity; it embodies the creative nature of our art. It unifies vulnerability and spontaneity; it uses the whole instrument—mind, body, and heart; and when we speak, we seldom think about how we sound—we just do it.

The Stradivarius and "Technique"

I don't like the term *technique* because it suggests something mechanical. But for lack of a better term I use it to mean the things we do to produce sound. Good technique is crucial, as I often demonstrate in an analogy about Stradivarius violins.

Most people have heard of Stradivarius violins. These instruments deserve their reputation as the best of the best, but their fame has little to do with the quality of the bow or the string. The quality of a Stradivarius comes from its resonator—the kind of wood it is made of, its shape, how long it is seasoned, and so on. When all of those things are at an optimum level, the violin gets the sweetest, most resonant response to the action of the bow and the vibration of the string. Different qualities of bow and string make a difference, but it is primarily the resonator of the instrument that defines the quality, and the refinement of that resonance is the key to the Stradivarius's fame.

Here is the plug for technique: Give me a Stradivarius with the finest bow and string available to play, and it will sound scratchy and terrible because I have no violin technique. But put a cheap rental violin in the hands of a top-flight violinist, and it will sound fabulous. The crucial difference is much more in how one uses the instrument than in the quality of the instrument itself.

The voice is the case in point. We hear all the time, "Wow, he has such a great voice—a wonderful instrument!" How do we really know that? The vocal folds of a great singer, compared to those of somebody who can't carry a tune, appear very similar. The big difference is in the use of the instrument. The reason people say someone has a wonderful voice is that the way that person instinctively uses his or her voice produces a rich, beautiful sound. To varying degrees, some people make beautiful sounds by instinct, imitation, or nature, but most of us must learn it by nurture—we have to be taught. Singers can imitate or manufacture good tones, which will make people say they have a good voice, but again, the difference is not so much in the instrument as in how that instrument is used.

This is not to say there are no differences between vocal folds—there are, of course, differences in length and thickness. Some vocal folds are so strong they can be abused day after day and still seem to "keep ticking." Other vocal folds can be mildly abused and develop nodules or even rupture. Not all vocal folds are created equal, but even those seemingly indestructible voices would sound better if used more efficiently. Vocal folds do differ slightly from singer to singer, but the sound quality and longevity of the voice depends more on the use of the voice than on the physical gift of the singer.

People who have lesser vocal gifts must sing better, whereas those with the greatest vocal gifts don't have to sing as well because their instruments can take more abuse. That presents a challenge because we often model our singing after those who have the greatest vocal gifts but often are poor technicians.

To reiterate: There are differences between instruments, but the more important difference is in how people use their instruments.

The performing arts differ fundamentally from the visual arts. A painter's creative work happens when he or she is alone in the studio. When finished, the painting is framed and hung on the wall. People are affected by it after it has become static and fixed—a museum piece. Performing art happens as we move through time, and audiences are affected as the art is being created.

Singers tend to think of technique as if it were a painting, as if all the creative work is done in the practice room alone. With this mentality, when a tenor "hits" a high C, he is not in the moment at all; he simply displays the painting of the high C that he worked out in the practice room. It is common for singers to "phone in" performances—not "being in the moment" of their performance or creating something fresh and new. Displaying the painting is contrary to the fundamental nature of the singing art.

Because singing must be constantly created in the moment, we must have a technique for it that moves through time as well. Good technique is *not knowing* what is going to happen when we sing; rather, it is being very clear and sure about what we are *doing* and the parameters in which those actions occur. Just like a professional ice skater is in constant motion, singing must be constantly moving and changing. Skaters don't gain stability by standing still—they constantly flow and move around the ice. They move through time. They draw balance and strength from constant forward motion.

To maintain that sense of constant motion, one of my students imagines that he is walking on quicksand while singing. If he just stands fixed in one place, he will sink into the quicksand, but if he is constantly in motion, he will make it across safely. This same idea applies to an experience I had once while hiking to a high mountain peak in Colorado. I reached an area above the tree line where the steep slope was covered with loose gravel. If I stopped and stood still, I started to slide down the side of the mountain, but by continually moving forward I made it through that dangerous section to the firm ground on the other side.

These analogies point to the idea that great singing is not staid or stiff. In fact, the only way to find true stability and strength in singing is to let go of the illusion of stability (which usually leads to stagnation and tension). True strength and stability come from surrendering control, constantly moving forward, creating each moment, finding a groove, and flowing through it.

Evaluation is the opposite of movement. The left side of the brain analyzes and evaluates, making us stop and look back rather than move forward. (Jokingly, I tell my students that, like Lot's wife in the Bible, if they stop to look back and evaluate what happened while singing, they will turn into a pillar of salt.) There is a place for analysis and evaluation in learning to sing, but not *while* singing! We evaluate and judge during lessons and practice sessions before and after singing, but not during the singing itself. The left brain helps us learn the rhythms, notes, language, and vowel articulation when preparing a role, an aria, or a song. Once we are thoroughly prepared, we must let go of all analytical, evaluative processes and let the right brain's creative, emotional impulses take over and move us through time.

TAKE THE TRIP

In this way, performing is like taking a trip. If my wife and I decide to take a trip to Cancun, we will sit down together and look through maps, guidebooks, and tourist information. Then we'll book airfare, hotel, and a rental car. We will research possible things to do while there. If we have friends or acquaintances who have been to Cancun, we will get advice from them on what to do and see. Based on all of that information, we create a detailed plan for our trip.

But *planning* a trip to Cancun is much different than actually *taking* a trip to Cancun. Planning the trip can be fun, but it is a completely different experience than actually lying on the beach sipping piña coladas or swimming in the ocean. Once we have planned the entire trip, we must actually take the trip. Poor planning can create a very bad trip. Our family once went to Paris for Christmas and didn't plan what to do while we were there. Consequently, we spent most of our time asking each other what we should do, and by the time we made a decision, tickets were gone or there wasn't enough time to do what we had decided. We ended up being bored and miserable most of the time.

Also, a trip doesn't always turn out the way we planned it. We can make all kinds of plans for the trip to Cancun and then get on the plane and have everything go wrong—we lose our ID or travelers' checks or have the wrong hotel reservations. When that happens, we must acknowledge the obstacles, find a good solution, and continue on the trip. After the trip, we evaluate what happened and make plans for a better trip next time around.

I work with a soprano who is very analytical and critical of her own singing. I tell her that she needs to quit evaluating and just take the trip. I say to her, "You make appropriate plans but never take the trip. As soon as you start to sing, you decide you don't like the airline and want to jump off the plane." When she doesn't follow through or move ahead with the trip, her voice sounds stiff and tense. For the sound to have life, we must not evaluate while taking the trip. We should only evaluate when the singing is done. When singers finish singing a phrase or performance, they will remember what the experience was like and be able to make more appropriate plans for the next phrase or performance.

People often live their whole lives this way. Instead of doing what they have planned, they give up, don't follow through or fail to adjust when plans fall through. Part of my philosophy of singing is that we continually learn from our mistakes—we don't get stuck fretting about a rejection letter or a mediocre audition. Those things happen to everyone. We should learn from mistakes and improve our preparation for the next performance opportunity. We will continually face the same problem until we figure out what we are supposed to learn from it.

> My biggest challenge is that I tend to overanalyze my work, even while singing. I have adopted the mantra, 'Think about singing before and after, but not during.' I don't always succeed in this, but the better I do in thinking before and after, but not during, the better I sing.
>
> Ferris Allen, baritone

This brings up one more angle on the trip metaphor: It is possible to salvage a bad trip. If things are going terribly wrong, we are better off to make the most of the trip. This is very difficult for many singers. When something goes wrong early in a phrase or performance, we often give up and everything afterward goes badly as well. We must learn to fix as we move on—salvage the trip—and save the self-criticism and evaluation for after the trip is over.

Lack of evaluation makes us feel vulnerable. Moving forward, following through with our plans is scary because we don't really know what the outcome is going to be. However, this kind of vulnerability is the essence of our art; it is how we uncover the naked voice. This process of opening up is what I call self-actualization—understanding more clearly and deeply how we think and function. Self-actualization in singing is somewhat like gradually taking off one's clothes, becoming more vulnerable, open, and naked.

As a singer opens up, it feels like another layer of clothing has been stripped away. While working on an exercise that freed her voice, a mezzo-soprano student of mine said during a lesson, "Well, there went my bra!" It was a hilarious moment, but it clearly conveyed her feeling that she was accessing her naked voice, that she had little left to hide.

Vulnerability and emotional honesty are crucial to our art. People can be impressed by good sounds, but something far more important happens when a singer combines impressive technique with emotional truth: Listeners are changed. A free voice opens a direct conduit from the singer's heart to the people in the audience. That is what singing should always be about. Fortunately, there is so much passion and drama inherent in operatic music that we can be moved despite a somewhat mechanical performance. But singers have the potential to do so much more than impress—they can help us transcend the mundane and teach us truths about ourselves that we might not otherwise have discovered. When singers achieve true vocal freedom, there is almost no end to the amount of good they can do—both in the music world and the real world outside the concert hall.

Superb musical art is disciplined and well prepared. However, the superb musical artist performs as if each note is being conceived for the first time. Singers have the additional obligation to perform as if each textual or dramatic idea is being conceived for the first time.

Vulnerability, spontaneity, constant motion, and creativity are essential to good vocal technique. The key to that technique is to return to the basic instincts of breathing and speaking. It is the gestalt concept of speaking that taps into our original creative impulses and enables us to communicate straight from the heart—with freedom, honesty, and power.

2

On Speaking

Speaking is innate to the human condition; we all do it. It is also the original creative activity. We phonate from the moment of birth, when we come scream-ing from our mother's womb. Doctors and midwives worry if a baby doesn't cry very quickly after birth because in that context, phonation is literally a sign of life (it is also one of the most beautiful sounds in the world). The baby's first action in life—after taking its first breath—is to phonate, to express fear at being thrust into a new world or to react to the pain, discomfort, and confu-sion of the birthing process. That compulsion to communicate—the need to express—is what I call the *source of utterance.*

The source of utterance is the basic idea, emotion, or thought deep in our souls that must find a mode of expression. As we grow up, that source, ini-tially expressed through crying, evolves into speech. Speech begins early, as a child experiments with various sounds in addition to crying. A mother often knows within a few weeks after her baby's birth if the baby is wet or hungry, tired or hurt, just by the sound of the crying. Other people hear only crying, but because the mother listens more intently (and perhaps with more than just her ears), she knows the subtle differences and can therefore meet her baby's specific needs.

Soon crying evolves into babbling, speech-like sounds that thrill relatives and friends. Children perceive that those babbling sounds make everyone in their world happy, so they continue to refine and specify those sounds, which eventually develop into speech. They learn to make words by imitating the sounds they hear around them, and they get encouragement and positive reinforcement for doing so. When children begin babbling, they are not discouraged from this activity. Instead, everyone encourages the failing, babbling efforts until they sound like words—clear speech.

As children speak words correctly and have their efforts affirmed, a pattern of speech becomes deeply ingrained. Normally developing children will learn to speak their native language fluently by the time they are four or five years old. By that age, the original source of utterance, first expressed through crying, has evolved from speech-like patterns into actual speech with a growing vocabulary and specific meanings assigned to certain sounds.

This process seems completely natural—the simple process of environmental adaptation. We learn at a very early age that we have needs and that by using specific speech sounds, we can get what we want from the people around us. We learn that we can even manipulate people with those sounds. At that early age, speech is totally self-centered—serving only as a means by which our needs are met.

Almost everyone naturally learns to speak efficiently. In other words, few people speak naturally in a way that harms the voice. Throat doctors tell stories of children who damage their voices through misuse, usually from screaming or in temper tantrums. Also, some children with hearing problems tend to scream when they speak because they think they will not be heard otherwise. But these are the exceptions—most people learn to speak with relative efficiency and at a comfort level that is free from strain or vocal harm.

Speaking engages all aspects of our humanity. When we speak, we involve our physical, acoustical, spiritual, emotional, and psychological selves. It is acoustical because we make sounds to do it; it is physical because specific tissues vibrate to make those sounds in addition to engaging the lungs, diaphragm, and articulators. Speech is also communicative, emotional, psychological, and spiritual because who we are—our beliefs, thoughts, feelings, and hang-ups—all affect speech and are communicated through speech.

The complex process of speaking has many parts, but in this book we examine those parts in relationship to the whole (hence, the Wholistic Approach). Speaking is a perfect parallel for singing in that we rarely think about all its various components or the physiological process to do it; instead, when we have something to say, we just open our mouths and speak—which is exactly what we should do to sing.

We normally don't evaluate the sounds we make when speaking. We think only about expressing ourselves or communicating an idea. Of course, speaking does produce sounds, and through those sounds we communicate, but the sounds per se are not foremost in our minds when we speak. By contrast, classical singers almost always focus on the quality of the sounds they make. We were given vocal cords and the ability to phonate for one primary purpose: to communicate. So when singers turn singing into mere sound making, they distance themselves from the source of utterance.

SIMPLY COMPLEX SPEECH

At first glance, speaking seems very simple, but it is actually an extremely complex, multilayered process. In addition to the basic purpose of communication, speaking involves the acoustics of sound production, muscular engaging of the vocal folds, movement of the articulators, the mechanics of breathing, and the intricacies of inflection or tone. The tone of voice often communicates far more than words. For example, many people, when asked, "How are you?" respond that they are "fine," but the way in which they say "fine" communicates the exact opposite. Depending on the inflection, "fine" could mean bored, angry, depressed, hurt, smug, embarrassed, or any number of emotions that are not inherent in the meaning of the word itself. We convey so much through the *way* we speak that when we consider everything involved, speaking becomes profoundly complex.

Speaking requires no talent. It comes so naturally and organically that most people don't see it as creative. But every time we speak, we create something—a word or an expression of meaning or emotion—through phonation, the simple vibration of our vocal folds.

Because we normally do not pay much attention to the sound of the voice when we speak, we are often shocked by the sound of our own voice on tape. Inside our heads we hear ourselves differently than others hear us. Also, we usually don't notice our own regional dialects, accents, or inflections unless we hear our voices on tape. Just as we don't pay attention to how speaking sounds, we should similarly not pay attention to how it sounds when we sing.

However, while learning to sing, we typically *do* pay a lot of attention to the sounds we make. We listen for balance, clarity, vibrato, pitch, beauty, and the freedom in the sound, but we don't necessarily think about what causes the sound or why it is so natural and easy. We must understand and be conscious of the original source of utterance so that when we sing, we do it with the same ease and subconscious freedom that we have when speaking. That way, the beautiful sounds will always communicate a specific intent or emotional truth.

But that is the endgame. With my students, I begin by stripping away emotional intent and accessing the core speaking voice. I ask them simply to speak, without intention or meaning. For example, in the very first exercise, we speak five pure vowels preceded by the "n" consonant, without any expressive or communicative intent. By doing this, we sense the constant buzzing vibration of the voice, and we come to understand that we must continually create that vibration to speak.

ENVIRONMENTAL CONTAMINANTS OF SPEECH

We learn to speak by adapting to the sounds and expectations of our environment. As we grow older, the way we speak leaves an impression on listeners. For example, we might consider a woman an "airhead" if her voice is high and airy. The stronger a person's voice, the stronger and more confident we consider that person to be. Some people may have contaminated speech patterns if they were raised in emotionally constrained circumstances where they were expected to speak and act a certain way to be considered acceptable. The deep connection between speaking and self-identity exemplifies how intimately speaking is connected to all the various parts of our humanity and how societal pressures can corrupt or obstruct our ability to connect with the original source of utterance.

One of my students had serious issues with environmentally contaminated speech, which directly affected her singing. She was a professional actress, and while performing onstage, her speaking was clear and fluid. But in regular conversation, her speech was halted and tense. She had been taught to be careful choosing her words and expressing herself, so she constantly checked herself to make sure her words came out exactly right. I observed that she did not feel confident or secure when being herself, but when acting, she felt free to communicate clearly and fluidly. She was totally vested and healthy in stage acting. However, because she spoke a lot more in everyday life than she did onstage, her voice always seemed to be in trauma.

Part of the problem was that her receptionist job required her to speak in a very reserved, stilted way. Her singing was more like her halting conversational speech. I found the key to help her singing only after hearing her perform a straight dramatic role—I asked her to use her stage speech as the way to speak for singing. She eventually realized that her everyday speech was stiff and halted. She applied the "stage voice" to her singing, and everything improved.

She was an exceptional case. I often find that the best way to help people reconnect with the original source of utterance is to get them to speak in what I refer to as vernacular speech, using the sounds, accents, and idiosyncrasies of their original, native tongue. This is easy for most people because it is difficult to eradicate the deeply ingrained patterns of vernacular speech. I know people from Texas who have lived in New York City for forty-five years and still speak "Texan." I also know people from the Bronx who live in Texas yet still speak with a Bronx accent. I had a friend from England who originally learned to speak with a Cockney accent, and even after forty years in Oklahoma, his speech still retained traces of Cockney. The basic patterns of vernacular speech are so deeply ingrained that it is difficult to eradicate them completely, and when we do, I think it separates us from our most authentic selves. That is why when I teach, I begin by having my students speak simply and in their own vernacular.

Vernacular speech is not truly natural (i.e., we are not born with an Arkansas or Cockney accent); we acquire a vernacular speech pattern by adapting to our environment. Yet because that subconscious process of adaptation is slow and supported by constant positive reinforcement from the people around us, it seems like the most natural and honest way of speaking. If we depart from the vernacular, we feel pretentious and fake.

When people move into more important positions in life, they sometimes purposefully change the way they speak to make a specific kind of impression. I've read about business leaders from the American South who take classes to eliminate their drawl because some people make negative assumptions about the intelligence of a person who speaks with a drawl.

I met someone a few years ago who is originally from the South. I was surprised to discover he was from the South because he spoke with a quasi-British accent and had wiped out any audible trace of his Southern upbringing. Interestingly, he seemed distant and aloof when I met him. I wondered if the process of distancing himself from his Southern upbringing had disconnected him from his most authentic self.

Beginning with Vernacular Speech

Whether conscious or subconscious, vernacular speech can become corrupted and contaminated, which normally inhibits vocal freedom and obstructs access to the original source of utterance. That is why, in this approach to singing, we begin by using vernacular speaking—not speaking the way we think we should, but in the way we naturally learned to speak through our early years. When we speak in the vernacular, we move the articulators (jaw, tongue, lips, and pharynx) relatively easily and efficiently because we aren't conscious of them. We simply imitate the sounds around us without being conscious of how they are moving.

Vernacular speech, however, is only the beginning point. It has less potential for dynamic expression and pitch variation than is required for classical singing. Also, elements of vernacular speech entangle the muscles around the voice, so eventually we must refine the movement of our articulators beyond vernacular speech to achieve complete freedom. In this way, learning to sing is like learning to speak all over again. We begin by getting the voice to speak cleanly and clearly, without any kind of fakery or pretension. Then we gradually learn to articulate the vowels much more specifically than we do in regular speech. By doing so, we find the vital core of the voice, but naturally, without the sound of pretension and pressure often associated with classical singing. To hear a comparison of vernacular speech to refined speech, listen to Audio Sample 1.

 AUDIO SAMPLE 1: Comparison of Vernacular and Refined Speech

I use the term "core" because it implies the essence or center of something, as if the voice is stripped naked, without any decorations—like a Christmas tree without the lights and ornaments. I want to hear the core of the voice when someone speaks or sings. I find that when people access the core of their voice in speaking, they often reconnect with their authentic selves as well. Simple, unadorned vernacular speech is the way we connect with that original source of utterance, the need to express and communicate, which is in the end, the whole point of learning how to sing.

3

On Breathing

Breath is the essence of life. Images of breath as a life force permeate language, religion, poetry, philosophy, and science. The book of Genesis says that when God created man He breathed into him the "breath of life," and man became a living soul. Many religions use a form of meditation in which a person focuses simply on breathing to find the center or essence of the soul on the path to enlightenment. To scream at birth, a baby must first take a breath. Breath is much more than just bringing air into the lungs and letting it out again—the breath of air is specifically and inextricably connected to our bodies. Breath links us to the source of life itself.

Before the birth of our two daughters, my wife and I attended natural child-birth classes, where we learned that the most important preparation for natural childbirth was learning how to breathe. When contractions begin, the mother's breathing must have a steady flow in and out. This steady breath flow mitigates the intense pain when the muscles in and around the uterus contract. The mother's natural reaction to that searing pain is to hold her breath, but the more she holds her breath, the more pain she will have. Maintaining a consistent flow of breath isolates the hard, contracting uterus; otherwise, the woman pushes against the pain, which tightens the muscles all around the uterus, increases the pain, and debilitates the entire body.

Breathing is involuntary. When healthy, living people inhale, oxygen enters the bloodstream and supplies life to the rest of the body. If a tourniquet is placed too tightly around a specific body part, the oxygenated blood will stop flowing to that part, and it will die. Breathing is literally an essential part of life, with profound implications as big as life and death. Through breathing, we calm our emotions, eliminate pain, focus our minds, and connect to our souls.

Breathing and speaking are the two active ingredients in singing, and it is in the process of understanding the essence of those two ingredients—getting them to function in coordination and alignment with each other—that we find our authentic, naked voice.

APPROACHES TO BREATHING

There are almost as many ideas about correct breathing for singing as there are voice teachers. Every vocal pedagogy book has a chapter about breathing, and the various approaches range from "Don't think about breathing at all," to the most complicated and intricate understanding of the musculature involved and how to manipulate the muscles for proper breath support. The latter approach focuses on the use of intercostal muscles, expansion of the rib cage, use of the pelvic muscles, and raising the chest. Although none of those things is necessarily wrong (indeed, some of those ideas are provably correct by scientific measurement), they are simply descriptions of what *happens* when we sing correctly, not what we *do* to sing right.

In normal conversational speech we don't think about breathing at all, yet every breath we take while speaking is a preparation for the next moment of speech. We are generally not conscious of that preparatory breath. For example, one would not walk into a room and take a big breath to say, "Hi, Steve. How are you?" For that short phrase we need hardly any breath at all. However, if I lose my temper and go on a tirade, I take a huge breath before screaming at the person who upset me. Somehow we instinctively know that to speak with a high level of emotion and power, we must take a big breath. In that emotionally charged moment, we never consciously think, "I am about to go on a tirade, so let me make sure I get a big breath." Because we know what we are about to say, we automatically take enough breath to finish the phrase. We also know subconsciously that if we don't breathe deeply, we will run out of air, the voice will tighten, and we will not finish what we wanted to say.

The more simply we think about breathing, the better we will do it. However, correct breathing is not so simplistic that we don't think about it at all. To have the kind of power necessary for singing, the voice must speak clearly, which creates an intense muscular vibration. To balance and buoy that intensity, the breath must flow freely and consistently, which requires intense engagement with the breathing process. While singing, we cannot forget about breathing altogether, but we must not focus too much on the physiology of breathing. With that caution in mind, I will explain, as simply as possible, the breathing process.

The image of a glass submersed in water and the water rushing into the glass as a picture of air filling my lungs helped me understand that air fills my lungs as soon as I drop my diaphragm without moving my chest, torso, shoulders or head.

Andrew Milligan, tenor

INHALATION/INSPIRATION

The major muscle of inspiration or inhalation is the diaphragm. (I prefer the term *inspiration* because it captures the idea of the breath inspiring what we are about to say, but I will also occasionally use *inhalation* interchangeably.) The diaphragm is located at the bottom of the rib cage—think of the rib cage as "encasing" the diaphragm. When relaxed, the diaphragm is dome-shaped, like a bowl turned upside down. When we inhale, the diaphragm tenses and flattens. This action naturally expands the bottom of the rib cage. To accommodate the lowering of the diaphragm, the abdomen should expand (see Figure 3.1). Additionally, above the diaphragm, the gauze-like material of the lungs expands to fill up the newly vacated space. That expansion of the lungs creates vacuum pockets that draw air through the mouth and/or nose, trachea, and bronchial tubes into the lungs. The lowering of the diaphragm causes all of that to happen.

Most trained singers inhale correctly because the process of proper inhalation seems to be widely understood and accepted in the singing world. However, I often need to teach proper inhalation to untrained adults. Sometime between infancy and adulthood, people commonly develop unnatural breathing habits. This might come from instructions like "Suck in your gut," or "Hold in your stomach," and the resulting onset of physical self-consciousness and vanity. Proper inhalation demands "pooching out the stomach" or abdominal expansion.

It is important to think about inhalation as an expansion of the abdomen, not the chest. Often when people are asked to take a big breath, they stick their chests up and out. Although it is true that the lungs are inside the chest cavity, and expanding that cavity in this way also expands the lungs, it is not the

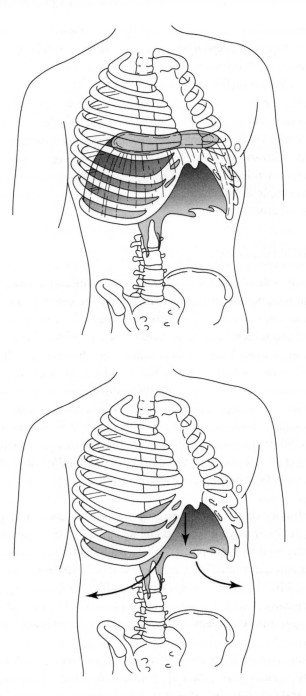

Figure 3.1. Contraction of the diaphragm and expansion of lower abdomen for inhalation

best way to breathe. Lower abdominal expansion naturally fills the lungs as the diaphragm flattens. The key is to make the process as natural as possible. The best way to understand the natural breath process is to watch a sleeping baby breathe. A baby's stomach naturally "pooches out" to inhale and then relaxes to exhale.

Correct inhalation, however, involves much more than just expanding the stomach. To get a good, deep breath for singing, we expand the whole lower abdominal region. Because the diaphragm is aligned with the bottom of the rib cage, it is higher in the front and lower in the back. Therefore, when the diaphragm flattens, the abdomen naturally expands more in the front, with some expansion in the back.

We must also have good body alignment to breathe correctly. The way I describe good body alignment is to imagine you are suspended in the air by a hook connected to the middle of the top of your head. Hanging from that hook, the body falls into proper alignment—the chin is not thrust forward or tucked into the neck, so the head rests comfortably over the rest of the body; the spine feels stretched but relaxed; the chest is pulled up, but the shoulders and arms dangle down at the side (see Figure 3.2). The most healthy, natural alignment is a high chest, a neutral spine, and an evenly balanced head.

Various techniques exist to improve body alignment. One of those is the Alexander Technique, which can be very helpful in aligning the body for all activities in life, including singing. It is particularly good for singing because it helps eliminate unnecessary tension.

Proper body alignment is absolutely necessary for free-flowing breath. If the body is aligned, the action of inhalation occurs only below the diaphragm. In fact, everything above the diaphragm is just a passageway for the air. There should be almost no muscular activity above the diaphragm in breathing because when the body is aligned, the chest will already be expanded as much as necessary. We can expand the chest to get more air, but that is not natural or efficient. The chest should neither expand nor collapse during proper inhalation or exhalation.

So when the diaphragm flattens for inspiration, it is tense. As it relaxes, it returns to its dome-shaped position and compresses the air out of the lungs in a reverse path through the bronchial tubes, trachea, and finally the mouth or nose. That is the basic process of respiration. In singing, that process is enhanced for the simple reason that the voice vibrates on a wider pitch range, requiring more energy and intensity in the vocal folds, which are stretched much longer than they are for regular speech. Singing requires a bigger breath response, so we need to take a bigger breath than we normally would for speech.

Good   Bad

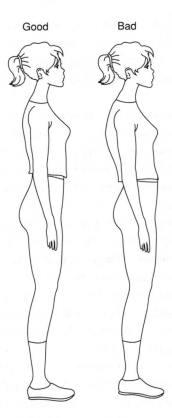

FIGURE 3.2. Proper body alignment

    That is the most clear, uncomplicated way I have found to teach inhalation for singing. Expanding the lower abdomen enables us to get a better breath in the freest way possible, which then provides enough air to sing anything we want. Most people get the idea of inhalation pretty quickly and easily. The bigger problems emerge when dealing with exhalation.

EXHALATION

There are many approaches to dealing with exhalation. Because these approaches vary drastically, it is easy for a singer to become quite confused. They want to know, "Do I hold in? Do I push out? Do I lift and tuck?" Most complications with breathing stem from these contradictory ideas about exhalation, and it is precisely in this area that my approach might seem controversial.

I once taught a tenor in his late twenties who was having a decent professional career at a regional level. After a series of auditions, his manager advised him to do some vocal technique work based on feedback from the auditions that he had a certain reedy, edgy quality in his voice. Following that advice, he found me, and we began to work together on two main issues: First, he had a tense vocal production from trying to make a sound that was not his own, and second, he had major breathing issues.

> I have learned to breathe for the phrase, let the texts inspire the breath, and release the breath right before the beginning of each phrase rather than holding it. I used to take a huge breath for every phrase whether I needed it or not. I learned that I needed to trust that my breath was going to carry me through each phrase.
>
> Christine Brewer, soprano

After working together for a year, he came to the Aspen Music Festival for a summer to work with me as a participant in the chamber music program. Normally, each faculty member at Aspen gives a master class, and before my class he came up to me and confided that he was worried. When I asked why, he told me, "I like you and what you teach, but I am afraid other people will not like you because of your controversial ideas."

I was very surprised that he described my ideas this way. I asked him what exactly was controversial about the way I teach. I felt most of my basic information came from widely accepted sources—textbooks, National Association of Teachers of Singing (NATS) journals, or other voice teachers and were generally accepted. He answered, almost in a whisper, "Well, it's the way you teach breathing—it's very controversial!" I was shocked to hear that, because I felt my ideas about breathing were logical, obvious, and natural. Since that time I have discovered that he might have been right. My ideas about breathing are controversial because they fly in the face of one of the most revered concepts in vocal pedagogy—*breath support.*

THE S-WORD

I have been so vocal about my objection to the use of the word *support* that my students sometimes refer to it as "the s-word." If it were up to me, the word would be obliterated from the vocabulary of all voice teachers, coaches, conductors, and singers. My strong objection is due to the vocal production problems that arise out of the images this word evokes. The actions resulting from the use of the term *support* almost always cause increased air *pressure.* For singers to have freedom in their vocal production, they need greater airflow, not air pressure. It is a simple law of physics that the greater the air pressure, the less the airflow, and the greater the airflow, the less the air pressure.

Singers are typically told to inhale and then "support the tone from the diaphragm." This conjures the image of structural support, as a foundation supports a building or trusses support a bridge. In these cases, something is firm and strong and holds up something else. So in trying to "support from the diaphragm," singers typically tighten their abdominal muscles and thus restrict the free flow of air.

In a singer's formative stages, when the sound is thin and breathy, this abdominal tension results in a stronger sound due to overadducted vocal cords. Although developing strength of the vocal apparatus can result from this improper vocal function, it leads to a misunderstanding of the proper use of breath.

Students are often told to do multiple sit-ups every day to strengthen their support muscles. Strong abdominal muscles are not counterproductive to healthy vocal production, but stiffening those muscles while singing inhibits the flow of air. I am certainly a proponent of every muscle in the body being healthy and strong, but if those muscles are truly healthy and strong, we can relax and stretch them. If we consciously tighten the abdominal muscles as we would for a sit-up, we will sing with too much pressure.

Certainly some people mean airflow when they say "support." If the image that is always present in the use of the word is a Ping-Pong ball floating atop a fountain of water, then truly the flow of water is supporting the ball. The constant flow of air (or water, as in the Ping-Pong image) is what buoys the sound. But this image is seldom what the term *support* conjures.

It is true that to make any kind of tone, there must be resistance to the airflow. However, in efficient, free singing, that resistance should be only at the edges of the vocal folds. Because there are no nerve endings on the edges of the vocal folds, there ideally will be no *sensation* of resistance. Instead, there will be the *sensation of flow*.

RELEASING THE BREATH

After we take a good, deep breath (as in inspiration), we must release the breath so that it flows through the voice and out of our body. Releasing the breath is the most important concept in healthy, natural exhalation. When we train ourselves to inhale properly, the diaphragm flattens to a tense position, and the lower abdomen expands to full capacity. To exhale, we simply release all of the muscles of inhalation. If we truly release those muscles, the air flows out in one sudden motion. The air is not pushed out; we simply release the muscles of inhalation, and the air flows out freely.

Many people fear the idea of releasing the breath because they think releasing will collapse the chest or thoracic cavity. I do not mean by "releasing the breath" that once we inhale and expand the lower abdomen we just relax the whole body. If we do that, the upper body will collapse and we lose proper body alignment. Although we release the muscles we used to inhale, we always maintain proper body alignment.

When we release the air, the muscles in the abdominal cavity will return to their pre-inhalation state. That does not mean we squeeze or contract the abdomen; we simply release the expanded abdomen, and those muscles return to their original position. We are capable of contracting the abdomen without releasing any air. In fact, the more we contract the abdominal muscles while singing, the more resistance we will have to the flow of air. Remember Newton's third law of motion: For every action there is an equal and opposite reaction.

When we inhale correctly, it seems as if we are filling a reservoir in our abdominal area. This is not scientifically what happens, but when we inhale and expand deep into the pelvic region, that's what it feels like. With each breath we are either filling up the reservoir (if the previous phrase has depleted it) or refreshing the reservoir. When the reservoir is full, we don't have to pump it out or hold it in. As we release it, the vocal folds seem to siphon out what they need.

When singers tighten the abdominal muscles, thus holding back the air, I commonly ask, "What are you saving the air for?" We must nourish the voice by releasing the breath, not holding it back. If we restrain the breath by tightening the abdomen and not allowing the diaphragm to return to its relaxed position, we prevent the air from leaving the lungs and thus malnourish the voice. Because the vocal cords are capable of phonating with little air, strong voices can phonate and get the notes out despite being malnourished. But the voice will be much more colorful, vibrant, powerful, and free if the air is released.

The question always arises: "If I release all my abdominal muscles, and therefore all of my air, how will I sustain long phrases?" The answer is that while we are speaking or singing, the vocal folds regulate the exhalation of the air. They emit the amount of air necessary for the volume and pitch we are singing. So the paradox is, the more completely we release our air, if the vocal folds are vibrating efficiently, the longer our air will last.

My mantra about exhalation is: *Release all of your air, all the time.* This means not "controlling" that release of air. Singers are typically trained to gain *breath control*. I dislike the concept of *controlling* the breath because the vocal folds actually regulate (control) the airflow. Therefore, we don't need to control the breath. Proper exhalation gives us the feeling of being out of control.

Singers normally feel they need more support for high notes. Because the cords are tighter and longer for higher pitches, they do emit more puffs of air per second than lower pitches. This would lead us to believe that more airflow is required. However, because the cords are stretched long and tight for high pitches, they do not undulate as widely. Therefore, the volume of air in each puff is minimal. When we sing low notes, the vocal cords are short and relaxed, and there are fewer puffs of air per second. Because the cords are short and relaxed, the amount of undulation is greater; therefore, there is a greater volume of air per puff. So in free singing, the amount of air flowing through the voice (given a consistent dynamic level) is basically the same from high to low.

The concept of releasing the breath may at first seem controversial. However, when released while speaking or singing, the breath nourishes the voice in the most natural and authentic way. With this approach, speaking and singing become efficient and comfortable, and the resulting sounds become more vibrant and beautiful. Freely released air then allows the singer to connect to and communicate from the original source of utterance.

Part

II

THE INVENTIONS

Introduction to the Inventions

In the next six chapters, I explain the practical application of the philosophies of the Wholistic Approach to Singing I laid out in Part I by using six very practical, simple exercises that I call "Inventions." As I explained in the introduction, an Invention is something that takes existing materials and organizes them into a new form for a new use. In that spirit, I have taken the information I have gathered over the years about the function of the singing voice and gradually synthesized that information into six Inventions or exercises that enable singers to produce a beautiful, clear, resonant, and powerful sound with as much freedom and flexibility as possible. But before I explain the Inventions, I need to clarify some important concepts.

THE *CHIAROSCURO* BALANCE

One of the most important ideas we talk about in classical singing is achieving a chiaroscuro balance in the sound. The Italian word *chiaroscuro* literally means "bright-dark." Chapter 2 is about speaking, which I align with the *chiaro*, or bright part of the sound, and Chapter 3 is about breathing, which I align with the *oscuro*, or dark side of the sound. Our goal in singing is to bring these two ideas together to create a chiaroscuro balance.

As we progress through the Inventions, I frequently refer to the idea of creating a chiaroscuro balance. I will explain how the following terms are related and will use them as interchangeable synonyms:

speaking = phonation = *chiaro*
breathing = airflow = *oscuro*

I also frequently refer to *chiaro* and *oscuro* as opposite sides of the sound spectrum, and the Inventions follow a pattern of focusing on one side then the opposite side, then bringing them together to a balance, as follows:

First Invention: *Simply Speaking Simply*   Second Invention: *Free-Flowing Air*
(*chiaro*)   (*oscuro*)

Third Invention: *A Balancing Act*
(chiaroscuro)

Fourth Invention: *Spontaneous Combustion*   Fifth Invention: *The Wobble*
(*chiaro*—refined)   (*oscuro*—refined)

Sixth Invention: *Getting High*
(chiaroscuro)

Bright and dark are metaphorical opposites. In acoustical terms, I use *chiaro* in relationship to the fundamental tone and *oscuro* in relationship to the overtones and partials above the fundamental tone. There is nothing inherently exclusive about the production of *chiaro* and *oscuro* qualities in singing, but the typical way they are taught polarizes them.

Most conductors, voice teachers, and coaches try to help singers achieve a balanced sound. They want to hear both a brightness and darkness in the sound, but they tend to emphasize the *chiaro* quality because of its seeming ability to cut through an orchestra. Terms that are often used to describe that quality are brightness, core, focus, edge, ring, metal, singer's formant, ping, mask resonance, forward placement, *squillo*, bite, and cut. Each of these terms has different connotations in regard to vocal production, but all are attempts to describe the *chiaro* quality. The term I most often use to teach the *chiaro* concept is *core* because it evokes the essence or center of something, just as the core of an apple is its center. It is like an undecorated Christmas tree. Our core is the essence of who we are.

The terms most often associated with *oscuro* are color, resonance, richness, roundness, space, shimmer, spin, bloom, "opening up," and "making more room." Many singers try to get the *oscuro* sound by yawning, dropping the jaw, and imagining some kind of fruit in the back of the throat. All of these ideas aim for a sense of space in the back of the throat, but they often cause people to drop the jaw too far and push down on the voice with the base of the tongue. That might provide more color and resonance, but it also creates a manipulated sound and inhibits the flow of air.

I avoid telling singers to "make space" because that process usually makes *downward* space, whereas the correct, free resonance that gives spin and shimmer to the sound is mostly *upward* space. Of course, in physiological terms, space does not literally open up in the back of the head, but we do get the sensation of back space. That sensation provides the bloom or shimmer in the sound.

In the Inventions, I will give a very detailed technical explanation of how we condition the voice to produce a chiaroscuro balance throughout the vocal range. I have also included audio samples of several different singers doing the exercises in the Inventions—not as models for imitation, but as demonstrations of different voice types and singers dealing with technical issues and challenges.

The Qualifiers of Speech

Another important concept to discuss before launching into the Inventions is the four qualifiers of speech. Obviously there are differences between speaking and singing. These qualifiers come from the differences between normal conversational speech and the speech we use for singing. Those four qualifiers are:

1. *Projection.* In singing we must have more intensity than normal speech, which is not very intense and cannot be heard from far away. Also, normal conversational speech cannot sustain high pitches, so to be heard in a large hall and sustain high pitches, we learn to speak with projection.

2. *Line.* Speaking with line means speaking with constant intensity. Normally we speak with jerks, starts, and stops, but in singing we speak with a constant flow. This is not something that comes naturally to most people, so we have to learn how to speak with line. In musical terms, speaking with line is called *legato*. *Legato* is the Italian past

participle of *legare*, which means to bind or tie together. The practical definition of *legato* for our purposes is in a smooth, even style, without any noticeable break between the notes. I like to use the word *line* instead of *legato* because of the geometric image of an unbroken line going from one point to another with perfect continuity. If a line has no continuity, we call it a dotted or broken line, but the word line implies a clear beginning and a clear ending with continuity and forward movement in between.

3. *Defined vowels.* No one defines all vowels clearly when speaking, and we all have regional pronunciation issues (consider, for example the many regional pronunciations of the word *house*). So we must learn how to speak with clearly defined vowels. How we define our vowels affects the timbre (color) and resonance of the sound. In everyday speech, clear vowel definition is not necessary because the sounds go by so quickly. But in singing, vowel sounds are sustained over long periods of time, and to be able to define those sounds, we must have a more refined vowel definition. Also, consonants are by definition an interruption of sound, so we must also learn to pronounce consonants with minimal sound interruption.

4. *Our whole instrument.* By "our whole instrument," I mean everything in the body from the pelvic area to just above the eyes. When we breathe correctly, the breath extends into the pelvic area, and if sinus resonators are a part of our sound, then our instrument extends at least that high. In everyday conversational speech, we speak from the neck up. But if we try to speak with projection and line from the neck up, we will hurt ourselves and sound terrible. In speaking with projection and line, we must incorporate the whole body. Thinking of the whole body as the instrument also helps eliminate localized muscular effort. Good singing requires no localized muscular effort, but bad singing uses localized muscular effort in various locales such as the neck, the jaw, the tongue, or the abdomen. We *do* need muscular effort in singing, but we want that muscular effort to be efficient and evenly distributed to eliminate tension.

In chapter 4 we begin to apply these ideas and philosophies in actual exercises that enable us to speak with projection, with line, with clearly defined vowels, and with the use of our whole instrument. In subsequent chapters, we will learn about airflow and how we incorporate it into clear speech to create a balanced, chiaroscuro sound. Then we learn to sing a clean onset and release, develop flexibility, and explore the uppermost limits of the voice.

4

The First Invention: Simply Speaking Simply

The idea of Simply Speaking Simply is to learn to speak with clarity. In an ideal world, all of our actions and words would be free from the contamination of insecurity, fear, and ulterior motives. However, in the real world, we often don't speak with clear, direct, and honest intentions; instead, our words sometimes veil the truth we want to communicate, the emotions we truly want to express, or the needs we want the world to meet. Most of us are unaware of the ulterior motives that entangle our words, actions, and relationships. When we begin to look honestly at who we are and what we want and then access that most authentic part of ourselves, those entanglements become obvious. Seeing ourselves clearly, we have the power to change. Change brings freedom, and freedom enables us to speak with pure intention—the original source of utterance I discussed in Chapter 2.

Clearing away entanglements in our lives is a difficult, complicated process. Often it takes a gifted therapist or counselor to help us recognize them and eliminate them. In a similar way, I help singers access their most basic, natural voice, then try to free that voice from entanglements so it can speak with freedom and clarity. In Simply Speaking Simply, we learn to exclusively speak (not sing) without complications. I will explain that process in great detail. It is a complex technical process, but in the end, it enables the most pure and simple vocal expression.

The objective of this Invention is to isolate and fully exercise the muscles *inside* the voice box (intrinsic muscles). Isolating those muscles is difficult in singing because we often entangle the voice with muscles *outside* the voice box (extrinsic muscles). Entanglement of the extrinsic muscles causes pressure both from below the voice (*subglottal*, or below the glottis, the opening between the vocal folds) and above the voice (*supraglottal*). Singers often think subglottal pressure is correct because it feels like support, but, as I explained in Chapter 3, the word *support* is not helpful. What most people feel as support is actually subglottal pressure. That feeling must be eliminated.

We must also eliminate supraglottal pressure that results primarily from tension in the jaw and the tongue. The catch is that if we have supraglottal entanglement, we will have subglottal pressure also—they go hand in hand. To remove both, we focus on isolating the intrinsic muscles of the voice.

PHASE ONE: VERNACULAR SPEAKING

Free singing is less entangled than speech. However, we start with vernacular speech because it is usually less entangled than typical singing. Vernacular speaking means speaking our original language in the way we first learned to speak it, complete with all of our regional dialects and idiosyncrasies. In vernacular speech, we normally use the essential core of the voice, and in doing so, the intrinsic muscles of the larynx speak cleanly. This is what I call getting a clean, clear signal. I use the word "signal" to refer to the idea that a microphone has difficulty picking up a diffused signal but can pick up a clean one.

Classically trained singers sometimes have more trouble speaking in the vernacular because they have been trained to strengthen and enrich their voice, causing a pretentious sound. In this exercise, we seek to strip away that pretentiousness and uncover the essential core of the voice. For our best and most complete voice to emerge, we eventually have to eliminate environmental influences. However, the initial version of this exercise seems plain and ugly, and when we first find the natural center of the voice, it feels vulnerable and naked. That is an uncomfortable place to be for most singers, but it is essential in the pursuit of authentic, free singing.

In this chapter and elsewhere through the book I use symbols from the International Phonetic Alphabet (IPA) to denote the specific sounds below. Whenever the symbols are used, they will appear in brackets as indicated here.

Vowels

[i] = (h*e*)	[ɪ] = (s*i*t)	[ʌ] = (b*u*t - stressed)
[e] = (h*ey*)	[ɛ] = (b*e*t)	[ə] = (*a*bove – unstressed)
[ɑ] = (h*o*t)	[a] = (p*a*k the c*a*h – Boston)	[æ] = (s*a*t)
[o] = (s*o*)	[ɔ] = (*aw*l)	[œ] = (s*eu*l – French)
[u] = (s*ue*)	[ʊ] = (b*oo*k)	[ø] = (sch*ö*n – German)

Consonants

[b] = (*b*et)	[h] = (*h*at)	[n] = (*n*ow)
[tʃ] = (chur*ch*)	[dʒ] = (ju*dge*)	[ŋ] = (si*ng*)
[d] = (*d*id)	[k] = (*k*ite)	[p] = (*p*et)
[f] = (*f*ine)	[l] = (*l*ine)	[r] = (*r*ear)
[g] = (*g*one)	[m] = (*m*ine)	[t] = (*t*able)

French Nasal Vowels

[œ̃] = (br*un*)	[ɑ̃] = (ch*ant*)	[ɛ̃] = (s*ain*t)	[õ] = (l*ong*)

Classically trained singers often start off "intoning" sounds instead of simply speaking. An intoned sound is usually set at a higher pitch than natural speech and is often postured and somewhat tense. In the first phase of this Invention, we begin by saying [ni]-[ne]-[nɑ]-[no]-[nu] in our most natural, vernacular speech. This phase uses five pure vowels, preceded by the consonant [n]. I use [n] because it keeps the voice speaking and requires no movement of the lips or jaw and only a slight movement of the tip of the tongue. The order of the vowels progresses from the brightest to the darkest; this is typically considered the most forward to the most backward.

I begin this exercise by telling singers to speak without any kind of culture, to use plain, "blatty" speech. This discourages posturing the voice and trying to make the sound resonant or impressive. We avoid making a sound that is cultured or singer-like by using vernacular speech. Vernacular speech usually has less entanglement than most people's singing voices. Untrained singers usually start off speaking more simply, whereas classically trained singers are more likely to try to make a resonant tone through posturing and positioning.

But Simply Speaking Simply is the goal.

To begin this exercise, we should breathe as though we are going to speak, not sing. Trained singers often take in a huge breath before attempting this exercise, which can create too much subglottal pressure. Also, many singers hum the [n] at the beginning of the exercise, which usually causes supraglottal entanglement. Plain, simple, vernacular speaking with pure vowels eliminates most of these subglottal and supraglottal entanglements and helps isolate the intrinsic muscles of the voice.

I use two images to help isolate the activity of the intrinsic muscles of the voice. The first is to imagine a mouth on the larynx. People often do funky things with their mouths in an attempt to make their voices bigger or stronger. This practice infuses extraneous tensions into the voice. With the image of the mouth on the larynx, the energy seems to start in the voice and emanate outward, with minimal entanglement from below or above.

I also have people imagine a disembodied larynx that is activated by remote control. As in the previous image, the goal is to eliminate entanglements so that the voice speaks in total isolation. Similar to a beeper on vibrate mode, the voice seemingly begins to vibrate spontaneously, without any external pressure from breath support or tightness in the jaw or tongue. This image of the beeper is not so far removed from reality. Our brains send a neurological message to the voice, causing the muscles inside the larynx to begin vibrating. Therefore, the true generator for our instrument is the brain. This resultant action is the essence of Simply Speaking Simply. Listen to Audio Sample 2 for examples.

 AUDIO SAMPLE 2: Simple, Natural, Vernacular Speaking

PHASE TWO: SPEAKING WITH PROJECTION

Once we have established a relatively disentangled vibration of the vocal folds, we must learn to speak with projection. I usually get to this by telling the singer to say [ni]-[ne]-[nɑ]-[no]-[nu] as if talking to a person in the next room. This simply increases the intensity of the conversational speaking voice without adding unnecessary pressure.

In the introduction to the Inventions, I explained the four kinds of speech that we aim for in training the singing voice: (1) speaking with projection, (2) speaking with line, (3) speaking with clearly defined vowels, and (4) speaking with the whole instrument. We first speak with projection because our normal speaking voice lacks sufficient intensity. But when we project, our speaking becomes clearer. When the projected vowel is pure, it becomes clearer still. The key is to learn to project without entanglement.

Projection is a very important word. Typically, projection connotes using our regular voice but with more intensity and focus. I avoid telling people to speak louder because they tend to shout, which usually lifts the larynx, puts pressure on the voice, and spreads the sound. Shouting is not the same as projecting.

I want to avoid the idea that to speak with projection is only to speak louder, because loud usually means ugly or unpleasant. It is seldom a compliment to say a singer has a loud voice. Real projection is natural, relaxed conversational speech, but with more energy and focus. This enables us to be heard from far away without shouting or pushing. Projection maintains the essence of the authentic voice and is essential to getting the core of the voice to fully vibrate. Listen to Audio Sample 3 for examples.

 AUDIO SAMPLE 3: Speaking with Projection

PHASE THREE: SPEAKING WITH LINE

After learning to speak with projection, we must learn to speak with line. Musicians usually call this *legato*, but I prefer the phrase "speaking with line" because the word *line* captures a concept we have known since kindergarten: We line up for school, and we draw lines in art and math classes. A line starts at one point and ends at another, without interruption. If there is interruption, we qualify it as a broken or dotted line. However, *line* indicates continuity—a simple beginning, constant movement, and an ending.

All musical sound exists in a space of time. Speaking with line refers to the continuity of sound from one point in time to another. However, it is possible to make a continual sound between two points of time but not have true line. Speaking with line also requires almost equal intensity from one point to the next. Because our normal speech is full of inflection and undulation of intensity, speaking with line resembles monotone speech. We start with natural speech and add consistent intensity, which creates a sense of flow.

Speaking with line requires constant creative activity. Often singers begin this Invention correctly with a clear, disentangled muscular action, but then want to hold onto that action. However, speaking is a process in which the neurological impulse continually flows to the vibrator (the vocal folds). It is like an electrical current flowing constantly to an appliance making the appliance function. The neurological impulse, like the electrical current, constantly feeds the vibration of the voice, so it is spontaneous and new in each moment.

To demonstrate this, I will have a singer say [ɑ] and continue to speak it. There is an immediate vibration and muscular action in the vocal folds that continues until the singer stops saying [ɑ]. However, if the singer tries to hold onto the muscular action, and in so doing interrupts the creative process, the voice will get stiff and tight. It is possible to get a sound similar to speaking with line by driving the voice. But correctly speaking with line involves staying in the moment and constantly creating speech without driving the sound. This process seems to always have forward propulsion.

The continuous, spontaneous creation of projected speech is the key to speaking with line. It is a continual forward movement from one point to another. The idea of movement is fundamental to the concept of Simply Speaking Simply. Listen to Audio Sample 4 for examples.

 AUDIO SAMPLE 4: Speaking with Line

Phase Four: Speaking with Projection and Line on Pitch

When we begin this exercise, we speak in the vernacular, without any projection or line. But as we learn to speak with projection and line, the sound will approximate a pitch (a specific note on the piano keyboard). In most languages, certainly in English, sentences begin with high intensity and trail off, so the pitch descends at the end of the sentence. Speaking with line and projection eliminates this trailing off of intensity. In this phase of the exercise, I have the singer speak [ni]-[ne]-[nɑ]-[no]-[nu] with line and projection, and I find the pitch nearest to where the voice is speaking. This pitch is where we begin.

In our culture, women's speaking pitch normally falls somewhere between middle C (C4) and G3. Some women naturally talk slightly lower than that, but it is not common. Although there are no definitive rules regarding where certain voice types speak, I have found some consistent patterns. Women who

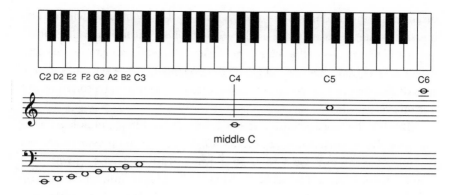

FIGURE 4.1. Keyboard and music staff diagram

speak at middle C are typically higher voices, such as coloratura sopranos. Women who speak at B3 are usually fuller lyric sopranos. Women who speak at B♭3 are generally dramatic sopranos or lyric mezzo-sopranos, and those who speak at A3, A♭3, or G3 are often dramatic mezzo-sopranos or contraltos (see Figure 4.1 for exact pitch designations).

Men have a much wider speaking range than women. The highest tenor I've ever worked with speaks comfortably at G3, but typically tenors will speak at F3, E3, or E♭3. Baritones normally speak at D3, C♯3, or C3, sometimes B2. Basses speak at B♭2, A2, A♭2, G2, or lower. One of my bass students actually speaks comfortably and correctly at F2. So the span of speaking pitches for all male voice types is about an octave, from F3 down to F2, whereas the span of speaking pitches for all female voice types is only about a fourth, from middle C (C4) down to G3.

I don't make a big deal about where someone speaks because the natural speaking pitch varies throughout the day, depending on the thickness of the vocal folds. However, knowing where the speaking voice normally falls, I can more easily tell if someone is trying to affect a higher or lower speaking voice and not speaking naturally. It is important that we try not to assign ourselves a specific pitch based on these categories. Rather, we just speak with line and find the pitch that most nearly matches our speaking.

After the first pitch is established, I move around the keyboard to random pitches, at least a third interval (two full steps) away from the original pitch, having the singer speak [ni]-[ne]-[nɑ]-[no]-[nu] on each pitch. I choose pitches randomly to maintain the spontaneity and constant creativity of the exercise. If two successive pitches are very close to each other, the singer will tend to anticipate that feeling and hold the feeling of the previous pitch. The distance and the randomness ensure a certain level of spontaneity without trying to replicate the sound made on the previous pitch. The feeling will be different in different ranges of the voice (if not on every note) because the vocal cords have a different thickness and length on different pitches. The key is to keep the speaking simple, free, disentangled, and constantly creative with projection and line on every pitch.

This is not a range extension exercise, so I stay within the middle range of the voice. Taken outside of that range, a singer tends to add pressure to access the notes. On this exercise, I never go above C5 with women or C4 with men (sometimes not even as high as B♭3 with basses). The lower limit for the exercise is no more than a third below their beginning pitch. Done successfully, this exercise consists solely in saying [ni]-[ne]-[nɑ]-[no]-[nu] on varying pitches while keeping the muscles in the larynx isolated and fully vibrating. Listen to Audio Sample 5 for examples.

 AUDIO SAMPLE 5: Speaking with Projection and Line on Pitch

PHASE FIVE: REFINING THE VOWELS

The next phase in isolating the muscles of the larynx is to purify the vowels. This takes natural vernacular speech to a higher level, which will be more refined and less entangled than natural speech. Because most people I teach have developed a higher level of hearing acuity, they can quickly progress to purer vowels. But even the most advanced singers must continually work to articulate their vowels with less entanglement.

The first common problem with vowel articulation is the *diphthong* (gliding from one vowel to another in the same syllable). Native English speakers use a diphthong for both the [e] (to [e:i]) and the [o] (to [o:u]) because we don't use a pure [e] or [o] in vernacular English.

But diphthongs are not the only challenge. Forming the vowels correctly, and therefore eliminating entanglements, gives us a clear signal. I recently taught a Swiss-German baritone whose voice sounded postured and fuzzy. He would say [ni]-[ne]-[nɑ]-[no]-[nu] with what I call "fake resonance" and could not get his voice disentangled. I had him speak in his native Swiss-German because in all of his training, he had been taught to use High German. I told him to think of a Swiss-German word that uses the [i] vowel, then the [e] vowel, and so on until he had a sentence that used all five vowels in his native speech. It took about a year to help him discover the core of his voice, but he finally unveiled his true voice by speaking in his vernacular with a clean, clear signal.

I have followed a similar process with many Americans because, in classical singing, there is a sense that we have to do it "right" and impress people, rather than just speak naturally. People from the Southern United States often have difficulty saying pure vowels, except for [ɑ]. In addition, the Southern dialect commonly uses diphthongs for [i] and [u]. People from the Midwest have the opposite problem—the [ɑ] vowel is overly bright (like [æ]), but the other vowels are clearer. Regardless of one's regional dialect, no one speaks with perfectly defined vowels. Therefore, everyone has to continually make adjustments to the articulators to disentangle the speaking voice.

To form pure, disentangled vowels, we must move the articulators (tongue, jaw, lips, and soft palate) in ways that are quite different from normal speech. For clearly defined vowels, the articulators must become more disentangled from the voice. To accomplish this, it is necessary to coax the articulators to function independently of each other, which is not typical of normal speech.

For example, with the [i] vowel, because the tongue is normally thrust high and forward in the mouth, the jaw closes to accommodate that movement. However, it is possible to keep the jaw in the [ɑ] position and move only the tongue to make the sound of an [i] vowel. So in this case, the jaw and the tongue function independently of each other. This articulation will feel very different from normal speech.

Refining the [i] Vowel

The [i] vowel is indigenous to every language in the world that I have heard; therefore, everyone seems to know how to say [i] without being told how to pronounce it. In the normal pronunciation of [i], the entire tongue, from the base to the tip, is thrust forward, the tip of the tongue touches the back of the lower front teeth and the arch of the tongue touches the front of the upper molars. The whole tongue is thrust forward, which causes tension in the base of the tongue and pulls the larynx up with it. We cannot get free phonation with the normal, forward-thrusted [i].

The key to speaking a free [i] is to let the jaw drop as if saying an [ɑ]. While saying [i] with the jaw in this position, the tip of the tongue may pull back from the back of the lower front teeth, the arch of the tongue moves farther back, and it touches the very back of the molars (see Figure 4.2). It is common when someone drops the jaw to the [ɑ] position and then tries to say [i], that

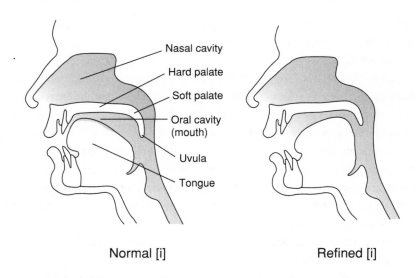

Normal [i]   Refined [i]

FIGURE 4.2. The articulators, normal and refined [i] position

the resulting sound is [ɪ] as in "bit." The singer must insist on the sound of [i], which requires the position of the arch to be farther back on the tongue. This position feels farther back than the normal [i], but the base of the tongue entangles the vocal cords much less. In this position, the arch of the tongue seems directly above the larynx.

Refining the [e] Vowel

The [e] is one of the most problematic vowels, simply because there are so many different versions of [e]. In fact, these multiple versions of [e] induced one premier French diction expert to devise a system to specify its many variations. English speakers tend to have more problems with [e] because our version always has a diphthong [e:i]. To eliminate the diphthong, most singers are often instructed to use the [ɛ] vowel, as in "bed" or "set." The problem with the [ɛ] is that the base of the tongue is typically low and spread, potentially creating greater entanglement.

I use a closed [e] because the tongue moves up and back more easily and naturally than with the open version. As with the [i], people tend to press the tongue forward instead of letting it move up and back. Moving from the [i] to the [e] is what I call the rolling effect, because the arch of the tongue lowers and allows the base of the tongue to move up and back. The refined [e] position feels

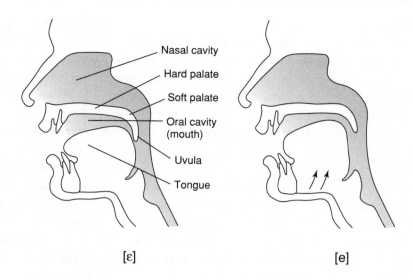

FIGURE 4.3. The articulators in [ɛ], and refined [e] position

very close to an [i] but is actually much more relaxed at the base of the tongue (see Figure 4.3).

Refining the [ɑ] Vowel

Some people may have noticed that I am using the [ɑ] rather than the [a] vowel. This is intentional. I feel that [a] entangles the phonation and resists airflow more than [ɑ]. The refined [ɑ] vowel has the least amount of entanglement of all the vowels, but it is also the most difficult to purify. We can say [i] and [e] with a great deal of tension in the tongue and the jaw, and they still sound like [i] and [e]. We can say [o] and [u] with a great deal of tension in the lips and the base of the tongue, and they will still sound like [o] and [u]. We cannot do so with the [ɑ] vowel. Any tension in the articulators while saying [ɑ] will contaminate the purity of the vowel. Also, [ɑ] is the most difficult to define because it has no specific tongue or lip position; therefore, it must be defined more aurally and visually. Ultimately, all vowels should be formed aurally and visually, but [ɑ] has to be aural and visual or it doesn't sound like [ɑ]. This is why I call [ɑ] a magically centered vowel—it is difficult to define, but once it is, all the other vowels fall into place.

As I mentioned earlier, [ɑ] is the only vowel that people from the Southern United States normally say well—they diphthong most other vowels. In contrast, people from the northern Midwest say the [ɑ] too brightly, in the direction of [æ]. The [ɑ] is sometimes coached with that Midwestern brightness to get focus and brilliance in the sound, usually with the justification that the French and Italian [a] have more brightness than the natural Southern American [ɑ]. However, that kind of brightness causes the tongue to press forward and tighten the sound.

One exercise I use to clarify the correct [ɑ] vowel is to contrast the vowels in what I call the "[ɑ]-family." I have the singer say the following vowels in succession: [ʌ] as in "hut," [ɔ] as in "awl," [ɑ] as in "hot" and [æ] as in "hat." This exercise can help people from the Midwest who might use an overly bright [ɑ] (similar to [æ]). I once taught a coloratura from Wisconsin to articulate a true [ɑ] with this exercise, and it revolutionized her singing. The important concept is that the changes in those four [ɑ]-family vowels happen inside—movement of the lips or jaw is not necessary, only movement of the tongue and soft palate.

When we say [ʌ] as in "hut," the base of the tongue and the soft palate are very low and relaxed. Thus relaxed, they drop down and deplete the richness and color in the sound. The [ɔ] raises the soft palate, but the base of the tongue stays low. For the [ɑ] the soft palate remains high, and the base of the tongue arches up. With the [æ] vowel the soft palate flattens, and although the base of the tongue remains high, it spreads and moves forward. The [æ] vowel is one of the ugliest and most difficult vowels to sing freely, often resulting in a flat quality and strident sound. The [ɑ] vowel is the ideal vowel to achieve balance because the high base of the tongue and the high soft palate allow the vocal folds to vibrate freely (see Figure 4.4).

Refining the [o] and [u] Vowels

The first three vowels, [i], [e], and [ɑ], require absolutely no movement in jaw and lips for the refined articulation. To further refine the [o] and [u] vowels, the only change from [ɑ] position is a movement of the lips. We commonly make the change from [ɑ] to [o] by dropping the jaw and the base of the tongue while slightly rounding the lips. However, this puts excessive downward pressure on the voice from the base of the tongue. The correct articulation of [o] is very different from normal speech. It entails keeping the base of the tongue up and high in the [ɑ] position, and then sliding the upper lip down over the teeth with a smaller movement in the lower lip. The [u] uses the same movement of the lips, just to a greater extent. In teaching this lip movement, I have my students picture a toothless person moving the lips to cover the gums. It is

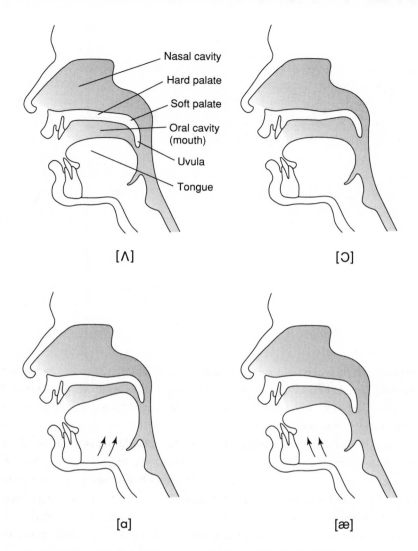

Nasal cavity
Hard palate
Soft palate
Oral cavity (mouth)
Uvula
Tongue

[ʌ]

[ɔ]

[ɑ]

[æ]

FIGURE 4.4. The articulators in the [ʌ], [ɔ], Refined [ɑ] and [æ] Position

important to note that this formation of the [o] and the [u]—simply moving the lips around a clear [ɑ] vowel—is drastically different from normal speech. It feels awkward at first, but it is ultimately the key to singing freely on [o] and [u] (see Figure 4.5).

In refining vowels, the ultimate goal is to train the articulators to function independently of each other, which doesn't happen in normal speech. In

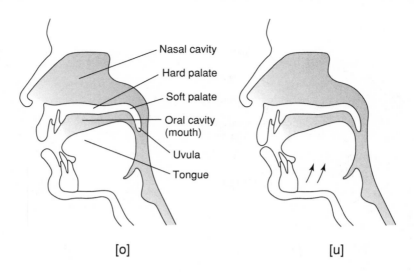

FIGURE 4.5. The articulators in refined [o] and [u] position

normal speech, when we raise the tongue to say [i] and [e] (tongue vowels), we close the jaw. When we round the lips to say [o] and [u] (lip vowels), we also close the jaw. Similarly, when we drop the jaw to say [ɑ], we usually press the base of the tongue down with it.

The key to achieving independence of the articulators is to always drop the jaw to where we naturally say [ɑ]. With the jaw in the [ɑ] position, we can say perfectly clear [i], [e], [o], and [u] vowels with absolutely no jaw movement. For free, disentangled, refined vowels, we must define those vowels only with the tongue, the lips, and the soft palate. The jaw can and should remain in the relaxed [ɑ] position—but not held—no matter what pitch or vowel we are singing.

This is an awkward process because it is so different from normal speech. People from any culture or language background must learn to purify and refine their vowels in this way. Depending on where they come from, people struggle with different vowels, but no one articulates pure, refined vowels in the vernacular. In time, the awkwardness wanes, and the refined articulation of the vowels comes to feel free, easy and natural. Simply Speaking Simply evolves from normal, vernacular speech to highly refined and purified vowels spoken with projection and line on various pitches. The process takes a long time to master, but ultimately it becomes the crucial foundation for everything that follows.

To speak clearly and freely, we must address the issue of the base of the tongue. Although it is not intentional, everyone initially tries to control the voice and make a clear sound by using the base of the tongue to help the adductor muscles squeeze the vocal folds more tightly together (see Figure 4.6). Simply Speaking Simply works toward eliminating any sense of control of the voice, achieving clear speech without rigidity in the base of the tongue.

If we tense the tongue in a downward, forward motion (the frog neck action), we can sense the size and strength of the tongue muscle. It is connected to the bone right behind the chin, all along the jawbone, and then connects to the windpipe (trachea) on either side of the larynx. Because the tongue is strong and completely fills this area, it is commonly used to control and manipulate the voice. All of us have used it for that purpose at some point.

Part of the challenge in speaking pure vowels is to eliminate tension and tightness in the base of the tongue. When free, the base of the tongue assumes a position that is up and back. When tense, the base of the tongue feels rigid and hard and seems to press down and forward. But if we release the base of the tongue, it will relax up and back, moving away from the vocal folds. This is a revolutionary step in enabling the voice to sing freely.

I had a poignant experience dealing with the base of the tongue when teaching Joyce DiDonato, a mezzo-soprano who began studying with me at the Houston Grand Opera Studio. She recounts that experience as follows:

It was my very first week in the Houston Opera Studio, and I was feeling quite on top of the world, having been accepted into such a prestigious program. Steve looked at me within ten minutes of beginning our first session, and said, "Joyce, you're talented and obviously very musical, but there is simply no future in the way you're singing. You're singing exclusively on youth and muscle." I was old enough (twenty-six years old) to trust that he just might be right. He then dug his thumb under my chin straight into the core of my tongue tension, which at the time was my favorite type of "support," and fought upward against the intense pressure I was applying downward, and he said, "now sing [ɑ]." I looked up to him, with the enormity of the situation slowly sinking in (what if the people at the Houston Grand Opera found out I didn't know the first thing about singing?), and I told him that I honestly could not phonate. I didn't know how to sing without the tongue muscle forcing the tone out. I could not manage the most simple of [ɑ] vowels without this crutch. I remember recoiling in horror at the situation, but deciding in that very moment to put my voice into his hands. We

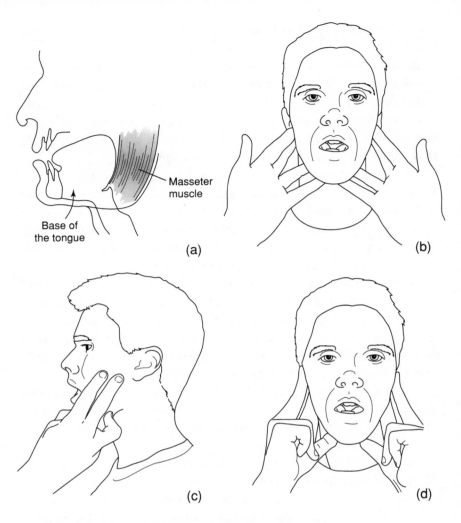

FIGURE 4.6. Tension in the Jaw and Base of the Tongue

then spent my entire first year in the program tearing down all the devices I had put firmly into place to aid me in sounding like an opera singer. The second year was then spent building up the natural, naked voice. Every single lesson was a breakthrough moment.

Joyce's process was indeed long and difficult. During that process she once performed at a house concert in Houston (a benefit for donors) where she sang "Non più mesta," an aria from Rossini's *La Cenerentola*, a role for which she is now rather famous. When she got to the high B at the end, her voice cracked, and the note "splattered" all over the place. When she told me about it, I was proud of her because this kind of cracking was an indication that she was releasing the tension in the base of the tongue.

Most people avoid cracking by holding onto that tension in the tongue, which prohibits bloom and freedom in the sound. The key is to let the voice always be cracked (i.e., no tension in the base of the tongue); that way, there is never anything to crack. So I say, "Get cracked and stay cracked!"

5

The Second Invention: Free-Flowing Air

In Simply Speaking Simply we learned to speak with a clean, clear sound, free from entanglements but with full engagement of the vocal folds. In Free-Flowing Air, we go to the other extreme, only minimally engaging the vocal folds so that the air flows freely and consistently in any range. We begin with a simple sigh and then build on that sensation in different ways to achieve a feeling of free-flowing air. Simply Speaking Simply isolates the *chiaro* or bright part of the sound; Free-Flowing Air isolates the *oscuro* or dark part of the sound. Neither extreme is a complete chiaroscuro sound, but by isolating them, we can fuse them together healthily later on.

THE PHYSIOLOGY OF FALSETTO

The body of the vocal fold is the *vocalis muscle* (see Figure 5.1). This muscle is covered by alternating layers of skin-type tissue and fluid. Commonly singers overadduct (squeeze the folds together). For overadducted folds to vibrate, singers must force air through with immense breath pressure. Free-Flowing Air takes the vocalis muscles out of the process, so we actually feel the breath flowing through the glottis without the sensation of resistance. The vocal folds

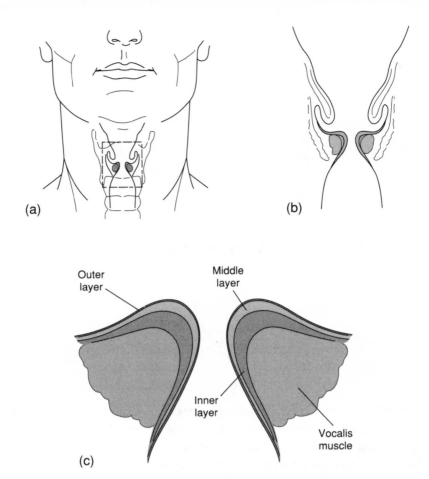

Outer
layer

Middle
layer

Inner
layer

Vocalis
muscle

(c)

FIGURE 5.1 (a), (b), (c). The vocal mechanism viewed from the front

are only slightly adducted, so when the air flows through, only the tissue on the outside of the fold vibrates—not the vocalis muscles.

This process is commonly referred to as *falsetto*. The "false" part of falsetto probably refers to the idea that a vocal sound only feels true and connected if the vocalis muscles are engaged. However, falsetto is actually a true part of the voice—it only feels false because the vocalis muscles are not engaged.

In chapter 4 I discussed proper breathing—we inhale, expand the lower abdomen, and then release to exhale. If we release the breath without making any sound, all the breath will flow out immediately. Because the cords are partially engaged in this Invention, there will be some resistance to the

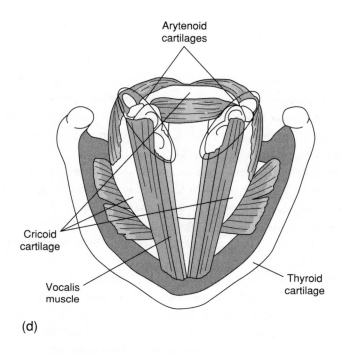

Arytenoid
cartilages

Cricoid
cartilage

Vocalis
muscle

Thyroid
cartilage

(d)

FIGURE 5.1 (d). The vocal mechanism viewed from above

airflow. The air flows out more gradually, but we do not control it; we actually release the air completely and allow the vocal folds to determine how fast it flows out.

In Free-Flowing Air, the air will flow out much faster than in full singing because the cords are not completely engaged. However, even in full singing it should still feel like we are releasing all of our breath all of the time. We actually *want* the sensation of losing our breath because that lets us surrender to the flow of air, thus feeling vulnerable and out of control. But in the process of letting go, we also gain the kind of power that only Free-Flowing Air can provide. It is common for singers to use intense muscular effort to make their voices sound bigger; however, in this Invention, we learn to let the airflow carry the sound, which in the end makes a much bigger sound with minimal muscular effort. As we condition our bodies and minds to surrender to the air and let it flow freely, our voices can open up to achieve the biggest and most beautiful sounds possible. Mastering this technique is a key to revealing the naked voice. And it all begins with a sigh.

We begin phase one with a vocalized "downward sigh." I use the word *sigh* because when we sigh, we release and expel the air freely, but with a hint of vocalism. The downward sigh starts in the upper, falsetto part of the voice, and we let the voice relax and the air flow out as the voice descends. We never consciously engage the voice, but rather let the voice go free as the air flows out. Any vocal response just happens on its own.

As I explained in Chapter 1, the vocal cords stretch longer for higher pitches. When the vocal folds are stretched longer, it is common to tighten them by squeezing them together (overadduction). Then, if the cords are overadducted, we will feel resistance and not be able to begin in falsetto. When we start in the upper part of the voice, we should have no sensation of air resistance. It should feel like falsetto.

Most men know what falsetto feels like. It is more difficult to introduce this concept to women because they seldom think they have a falsetto and are therefore not as likely to truly let the air carry their voice. With women, I use terms like "fluty," "choirboy voice," "dumb blonde voice," or "Julia Child voice" to help them achieve the feeling of falsetto. Women should try for a hooty, straight-toned, breathy feeling in the sigh without a feeling of stiffness in the throat. Women may confuse what is called "head voice" with falsetto, but what they think of as head voice is actually a mixture of head voice and a vibration of the vocalis muscles. Eliminating any vibration of the vocalis muscles is difficult but will result in a floating sensation and the feel of constant airflow through the voice.

Men often find falsetto much easier because it is a distinctly different feeling from normal speech. I have had a few students who claim to have no falsetto. One tenor in particular was adamant that he had no falsetto. I told him that yes, indeed, he did have falsetto; he just didn't know how to access it because of the tension he was putting on his voice. It took him a while to find the falsetto voice, but he was an exception to the rule—most men do so fairly easily. However, it is still common to overadduct, squeezing the arytenoid cartilages together (see Figure 5.1), but as with women, it should feel breathy, fluty, and hooty.

The challenge with men (more than with women) is that as they descend on a falsetto sigh, they often begin to squeeze the cords together again around a middle C or B3 to regain the sense of vibration and phonation. However, when done correctly with consistent airflow, the vocalis muscles should not vibrate until about an E3 for higher voices down to C3 for lower voices. In this exercise, all vibration of the vocal folds should be passive. We do not consciously engage the cords at all.

With women, the vocalis muscles don't start vibrating until about middle C or B3. The variation in pitch is less with women than with men (similar to the variation in speaking range). The important thing to remember in the downward sigh is to start in the upper register with a fluty, choirboy, falsetto voice and maintain that sensation to as low as is naturally possible.

We begin the sigh on an [o] vowel, and as we descend we try to keep the air flowing through that space to the lowest pitch possible while also retaining the sensation of falsetto as low as possible. The [o] vowel should relax the adductor muscles, which control the arytenoid cartilages. These muscles adduct, or close, the vocal folds. The adductor muscles are at the back (posterior) end of the cords and must remain relaxed. Because an [o] vowel resonates and opens up farther back, we are more likely to relax and open the back of the cords, where the adductors are.

If we hold the [o] position too low to maintain falsetto, we begin pressing the larynx low with the tongue and holding the vocal folds apart, which is just a different kind of resistance. So after the vibration comes back into the voice, we change the vowel to [ɑ] by relaxing the upper lip. The soft palate and the base of the tongue stay high in both [o] and [ɑ], so nothing in the back of the pharynx should change when we move from [o] to [ɑ]. We say [o] by simply pulling the upper lip down over the teeth.

This is all a complex way of saying that in phase one, we do a downward sigh with a sensation of falsetto to the lowest pitch possible. Listen to Audio Sample 6 for examples.

 AUDIO SAMPLE 6: The Downward Sigh

PHASE TWO: THE SIREN

In the second phase of this Invention, we begin with a reversal of phase one, going from low to high and then descending again. We begin on [ɑ] in the lower part of the voice, then slide up to an [o] in the upper part of the voice, and then descend, always maintaining the feeling of the sigh. I use the word *siren* in reference to the American ambulance siren, which swoops up and down in pitch. Even though we begin in the speaking range, the vocal folds should feel loose and flabby so that only the air passing through them causes them to vibrate passively. Again, we never actively engage the vocal cords in this exercise.

As we ascend in the siren, we begin on [ɑ] in speaking range and almost immediately take the voice out, gradually rounding the lips to create a fluty, breathy [o] as high as is comfortable and free. If we don't round to an [o] as we ascend in pitch, the sound tends to be diffused and spread. By rounding to an [o], the air stays directed and flows up and back with a free falsetto feeling and the sound stays clear and focused. Although it feels breathy, we are not striving for a breathy sound.

This phase of the Invention can be a coordination nightmare. We must simultaneously release all the air, keep the jaw and tongue in the [ɑ] position (the jaw is low; the back of the tongue is high), and gradually round the lips to an [o]. As the vocalis muscles gradually quit vibrating and move into the fluty, sigh feeling, the air continues to flow freely through the vocal cords. The key is to make sure there is no feeling of resistance to the airflow in the vocal cords at any point in this exercise. Coordinating all of these factors to maintain that airflow is not easy, but as we let the body go, releasing the air freely, as we ascend we get the sensation that more space is opening up in the back of the head.

The crucial point is not to think of space opening down (which causes tension in the jaw and tongue); instead, all the space opens up and back. This back space is key to the *oscuro* part of the sound. We do not make the space; rather, the airflow seems to give us the space when everything is coordinated right. This accomplishes one of the objectives of this exercise: to condition the flow of air to give us resonance room.

Back space seems to get "bad press" in the singing business. This is understandable because the normal way singers make back space is by retracting the tongue and pressing the larynx down. This kind of back space *deserves* bad press. However, the voice can never be free in the upper register or have real beauty without allowing this back space.

When we execute the siren correctly, we get the sensation that the space is gradually opening higher in the back of the head. I often use the analogy of a hot-air balloon to describe this sensation. As the air flows freely up into the back of the head, it fills the "hot-air balloon" in the back—an upward opening sensation. Another image I use is that of a parachute opening as the air catches it from beneath, buoyed by the constant upward flow of air. Like a parachute, we don't hold the back space open in an [o] position. We release the breath to an [o] and let the back space happen. The better we get at this, the more sensation of space we have and the higher that space seems to be, so much so that we feel like there is no ceiling to that air—it just flows right out of the top of the head. When singers begin to do this correctly, they sometimes get lightheaded and dizzy (as in hyperventilating). I sometimes tell my students that the additional oxygen in their brain might raise their IQ!

As we descend, we keep the air flowing through the [o] so that it stays heady and breathy to the lowest possible pitch, until the voice naturally comes back in (as in phase one). Often, as we ascend into the back space in this exercise, we close the jaw as we go up. To get the maximum color, resonance, and payoff in this process, we must keep the jaw in the lowered [ɑ] position and not close it as we round the lips into an [o] at the top. If we let the jaw stay open, there will be more space available for the air to buoy and fill in the back. The freer it feels, the freer it sounds—a freer voice makes a bigger sound.

Also, as we do this exercise, it is crucial to keep the vocal cords flabby and loose. The temptation as we ascend is always to add resistance to the airflow. When we start low in the speaking range, where the cords and larynx are relaxed, we keep that relaxed feeling as we ascend. The cords should feel flabby and loose into the highest extension of the voice. The key to this is keeping the jaw open and rounding the lips gradually into an [o] as we ascend. This allows us to keep the articulators in specific positions that will give the air direction. As we refine the articulation of the vowels, we can keep the function of the cords separate from the articulators without tightening or pressing on the cords. Refining the vowels, and thus narrowing the airflow, will give a healthy, true focus to the sound.

It's Not How High You Get

One of my mantras is *it's not how high you get that matters—it's how you get high*. In this exercise I do not care how high the pitch is, as long as people get there the right way—that is, without the sensation of resistance, with the airflow lifting the soft palate into a fluty, balloonish back space. Of course, the less resistance we have, the higher we will be able to go—but again, getting high is not really the point!

There are some common parameters for how high different voice types are usually able to go. Men often initially only go as high as F4 or F♯4, but as they proceed and let the air flow freely, they will eventually be able to do this exercise freely up to C5 or higher. Typically, low male voices are eventually able to get up to at least B4, and higher male voices often ascend to E5. As men perfect this exercise and give themselves over completely to the airflow, directing their air appropriately with the lips, with no resistance in the jaw or tongue, they can go even higher—sometimes up to an F5 or F♯5. Some high male voices can go up as high as a C6, but that is rare.

I must reiterate: Getting high is not the goal in this exercise. The goal is to get the sensation of free-flowing air. It is typically high enough if a tenor can get up to E♭5 and a bass can get up to C5 or B4. We go that high to make sure we get the sensation of being completely off the voice, so that it's all air and back space. Once we have mastered that sensation, going higher is not necessary.

With women I only go up to an F5, F♯5, or G5 because at those pitches they already have a heady sensation. If women go much higher than that, they tend to pinch the voice and not let the air flow freely.

Consistent Breath Flow

A common dilemma at this stage of the Invention is that people tend to give a surge of breath at the top of the siren. As they approach the peak, they surge as they go over and relax as they come down; however, the air must flow consistently from the bottom to the top and back down again. A surge of breath at the top will tighten the voice and create resistance to the air. If we keep the air flowing consistently into the hooty, choirboy space it will stay free, so we must allow the voice to always feel breathy.

Most people avoid breathy sounds because they do not project well. However, in this exercise, we are trying to get a breathy *sensation*, and sometimes this will cause a breathy sound. This is why when I hear tension in singers' voices, I tell them to let it feel breathier, to relax the vocal cords and let go of the tension. If we actually direct the airflow into the back space and let the voice feel breathy, we don't get a breathy sound. Instead, it comes out pure and clear—like a flute.

The flute is the only instrument I know of in which there is no particular substance that vibrates to make sound—only the column of air vibrates. This is why a flute tone is all overtones and resonance with almost no fundamental tone, and it is also why the flute is so relaxing. Although there are some exciting flute players in the world, the flute sound simply can't be as visceral and exciting as a trumpet or violin, both of which have vibrant fundamental tones. Thinking of the voice as a flute is useful in this exercise. Even though we make some sound as the air passes through the vocal folds, we feel no engagement of the folds and no fundamental tone at all—only overtones.

The Sensation of No Resistance

Another objective of this exercise is to train ourselves so that phonation can happen without any sensation of resistance. We do not fully phonate in this exercise, but we train ourselves to let the air flow freely through the vocal folds with a minimal sensation of resistance. If there were no resistance whatsoever, we would make no sound, and we do make sound in this exercise. However, we have the *sensation* that there is no resistance to the air. Because resistance is only at the edges of the vocal folds and there are no nerve endings in those edges, there will be no *sensation* of resistance. When we do the exercise correctly, we will feel no more resistance than regular exhalation.

As we siren up and down in this phase of the exercise, the peak of the siren should be higher with each attempt. As soon as we get so high that we start to resist, we should stop. In time the voice will be conditioned to let air flow freely up into the highest register without tension or resistance, but it takes time for that to happen, just as it takes time to condition the body for a marathon or Olympic event. This is not a quick-fix technique—it requires regular training and practice to improve, but the long-term results are lasting and healthy. Listen to Audio Sample 7 for examples.

> When I began this approach, I freaked out because I couldn't hear myself as well as I was accustomed to. My good friend Randy Behr had always said, "Either the singer hears himself or the audience does, and the audience *paid for a ticket.*" Steve assured me that even though I heard less, he heard a lot *more. I think it was then that I realized that to depend on feelings rather than sounds sets a greater standard of consistency and good singing.
>
> Josh Winograde, bass-baritone

 AUDIO SAMPLE 7: The Siren

PHASE THREE: THE DESCENDING FIVE-TONE SCALE

The pitch at the peak of the siren in phase two becomes the starting place for phase three of this Invention. The third phase begins like the second, in the speaking range. The voice slides up to the highest note reached in phase two, but instead of coming all the way back down, we descend on a five-tone scale (music example 5.1).

Let's suppose a singer gets up to G5 in phase two. In phase three she will ascend, sighing up to the G5, but instead of coming all the way back down, she will descend on G-F-E-D-C.

In the second phase we get a sense of expansion, opening up and back, and we want to keep that sense of space as we descend on these five tones. However, we don't keep the space by holding it in a certain position; instead,

MUSIC EXAMPLE 5.1. Free-Flowing Air

we keep it open by continuing to let the air flow into that space. This is a very important concept because most singers relax their articulators and airflow as they descend, which causes the soft palate, jaw, and back of the tongue to drop, adding tension and resistance to the airflow. If we keep the vowel concept (i.e., the articulators) active and the air flowing, the articulators will not drop down, and the air will flow continually up, back and high. The key in conditioning this into the voice is to continue to flow up and high when descending on the five-tone scale.

After the singer ascends up to a G and then descends on a five-tone scale, she begins again in her low speaking range, ascends up to an F♯, and once again descends on a five-tone scale. Then she ascends to F, descends on a five-tone scale, and so forth. As we proceed down by half-steps in this exercise, we come to about a fifth interval (three and a half steps) above where the voice starts to speak. At this point (around B3 to G3 for men or G4 for women), we just start at the top pitch, without sliding up.

The purpose of the slide up is to start where the larynx is relaxed in a low position so that as we ascend, there will be no tension or lifting in the larynx. By the time we get to a fifth above speaking range, there is no advantage to sliding up because the pitch is low enough that the larynx is typically relaxed and loose. So we start at the top pitch, maintaining a falsetto, fluty, airy feeling and descend gradually until the vocalis muscles begin to vibrate on their own.

We descend on an [o] vowel, and after the vocalis muscles start vibrating we change the vowel to [ɑ]; otherwise, it becomes necessary to force the vocal cords to stay open, which causes just as much tension as forcing them closed. Holding the cords open drops the larynx, along with the soft palate and the back of the tongue. The vibration of the vocal cords in this exercise is entirely passive. As we descend downward and the cords begin to vibrate, we must make sure that we are not actively engaging them.

Once the vocalis muscles are vibrating and we are proceeding down by half-steps, we think a new [ɑ] on each tone. By doing this, the tongue and soft palate will remain high, thus avoiding the common tendency to try to *hit* the low tone and make it strong. We must keep a high concept on each vowel, even as we descend. When done correctly, this process allows most people to sing much lower pitches than they would have thought possible. A voice with that kind of freedom can speak and vibrate much lower than normal because there is no downward pressure on the voice.

I typically say that women must be able to sing to C3 or else they really don't have the freedom they need. Most women find that idea shocking because they can normally get to G3 but not to C3. Obviously women don't need to develop those notes for performance, but the value of seeing how low one can go with this exercise develops a skill. For those

Extending the sigh exercise down into the extreme low register is incredibly beneficial. I'm a soprano, so this means vocalizing more than an octave lower than the range I actually use to perform, and the resulting sound is pretty comical. But this requires the ability to use a steady release of breath to set the vocal folds in motion when they are at their thickest and most relaxed. If I can't phonate clearly in this range, it signals to me that there is some sort of tension or entanglement restricting the vibration and shows me where I need to release things. The process of doing this exercise on a daily basis has cultivated a habit of always including steady airflow in my sound throughout my entire range rather than resorting to a straight "chest voice" on lower notes.

Claudia Friedlander, soprano

low notes to come out at all, we have to sing without any downward pressure on the voice and with a free release of air. The better we get at that release, the lower the voice can go. When the vocal cords are not pushed apart, they come together naturally with the flow of air.

Every woman I have ever taught has learned to descend at least to D3. Some women go as low as E♭2 without any pressure or pushing on the voice! And it is not always the case that the lowest sounding voices can go the lowest when singing. I've taught some mezzos and contraltos who consistently got to F2 or E2, but I taught a soubrette soprano who consistently got to E2. She simply grasped this concept early in her study and after a while, it was easy for her to descend that low. But again, it is not about how low we get any more than it is about how high we get—it is about *how* we get low. That said, I do encourage people to go as low as possible, simply because they can't sing those low pitches unless they do this exercise correctly. Listen to Audio Sample 8 for examples.

 AUDIO SAMPLE 8: The Sigh with Descending Five-Tone Scale

Nearly all men—even the highest tenor—can descend to F♯2 or F2. Lower voices and bigger tenor voices can usually descend to D2 and sometimes C2. A lot of basses and baritones can go so low that it doesn't even sound like a pitch—the cords come together so infrequently that it becomes difficult to distinguish the pitch. Several of my lower-voiced students descend as low as G1 or F1.

I taught a tenor at Juilliard who couldn't sing C3. As he learned to relax and let the sound come in naturally in the lower part of his voice, he found the correct pathway for the air. Now he consistently sings D2. Another tenor had a pretty, high sound but was inaudible lower than F3. After working on this exercise, he consistently descends to C2, and the middle of his voice is speaking clearly and beautifully. I once taught a tenor who had learned to sing great high notes by imitating recordings. However, he could not phonate lower than F3 because of the immense amount of tension in his voice. After much study, he was able to descend to A♭2.

> The Free-Flowing Air invention clarified something about which I had a good instinct, but I needed permission to allow myself to do something I thought was too easy to be right.
>
> Catherine Heraty, soprano

As I said before, how low we go is not important. It is important to descend to that lower part of the voice with a relaxed throat. We don't need those low notes for performance, but we do need the skill it takes to sing them. Acquiring that skill through consistent conditioning is one of the results of this phase of the Invention.

Over time, as we progress with this exercise and learn to direct the air in the right way, we will sense that the air stream is rather small, but it blooms in the back space. This can produce a full, spinning sound that seems very big. We are still not engaging the cords or getting any kind of resistance, but it can and often does make a bigger, fuller sound as we get better at it.

Making a big sound is, of course, not the objective—it is just what happens when we master this exercise. Also, the better our skill with this Invention, the higher we can go freely and easily. But we should not test the limits of our range in this exercise until we can go high with the voice being completely free, easy, and comfortable—otherwise, we just ingrain bad habits. I think this is worth repeating: It's not how high you get that matters—it's how you get high. This is a long and sometimes difficult process, but as we work on all three phases of this exercise, we can condition the voice so that the air instinctively flows along the correct path. That is the essential purpose of Free-Flowing Air.

6

The Third Invention: A Balancing Act

Singing, like life, is a struggle to find balance. Just as a pendulum swings back and forth to the extreme sides, its natural course is to finally settle in the balanced middle. For singers to find balance, they sometimes must go to the extreme opposite of what they are doing wrong. This is what I call "overcorrecting," and we often overcorrect so that ultimately we arrive in a balanced place. Singers who always sing with a bright, clear sound by squeezing the cords together have to be opened up for a while to focus on the darker, warmer back space that is the exact opposite of what they are accustomed to. The reason we overcorrect is to give singers the entire spectrum of possibilities so that they can find the balance in the middle of those extremes.

We are almost forced to find balance because the extremes just don't work in everyday life. Many people take the approach that if something is good, more is better. I have had a tendency to deal with one of my major personal challenges, eating, in this way. I love food. My normal approach to food is that if some is good, more is better, which is not a very healthy approach! The other extreme—starvation—is no less dangerous and can be fatal. For those who struggle with overeating, the great challenge in finding a balanced approach is that you can't quit cold turkey; food is necessary to sustain life. Alcoholics, smokers, and drug addicts can completely abstain and eventually live a completely normal and healthy life. Not so with food. With food you *must* learn moderation, finding a balance between the extremes of overeating and starvation. The challenge is to find that middle ground, a balance between extremes.

It is also important to seek balance because a strength can become a source of weakness. For example, I have known people who are extremely beautiful or handsome, which would seem like a good thing. But because of their physical attractiveness, they are often seen by others as sexual objects to conquer. This has made promiscuity an issue for some of them. In these cases a positive attribute became a source of struggle.

I have found it difficult to find a balance in always being honest. My natural tendency is to be honest with everyone around me, but I learned early in my life that not everyone wanted me to be completely honest with them—it was actually offensive to some people. What would seem to be a very positive quality actually became one of my worst, most offensive traits. I learned that not sharing everything I think and feel with people is not dishonest; I should only share my honesty with people who solicit it from me. I share complete honesty only with those who will take it in the right spirit and who want to hear it.

In singing, when we find that middle ground, the balance between the extremes of the sound, we get the most out of the voice. When the voice is balanced we get both a spectacular sound and a great deal of satisfaction from the freedom found therein. The Third Invention, A Balancing Act, combines the concepts of the First and Second Inventions with the intent to achieve a chiaroscuro balance in the sound. In the First Invention, we isolate the *chiaro* or bright quality of the sound by speaking with a clean, clear "signal"; in the Second, we isolate the *oscuro* or dark quality of the sound, using a sigh to achieve the sensation of airflow and open up back space. In this Invention, we blend these two concepts together.

The common approach to combining *chiaro* and *oscuro* is to squeeze the cords (for the *chiaro*) and then drop the jaw and press down the larynx (for the *oscuro*). That approach always produces an unbalanced sound because

> My biggest struggle with the Wholistic Approach was what I call the "pendulum effect." Because it works from the two ends of the vocal spectrum, I've found that I've had to try to find the middle point—between the spoken voice and the breath voice. During one lesson I would be much farther on the scale to only speaking the phrases without any breath moving; the following week, I would overcompensate and be very breathy, without the core in the sound. I think it takes a long time to let the pendulum really settle in the middle and move accordingly in the right direction, depending on where you are in the range.
>
> Joyce DiDonato, mezzo-soprano

those actions are mutually exclusive—they simply cannot coexist. After several decades of teaching, I have come to believe that the healthy, natural processes of Simply Speaking Simply and Free-Flowing Air are not mutually exclusive and that by fusing them together in A Balancing Act, we can achieve a fully balanced, beautiful, chiaroscuro sound without squeezing the cords together or pushing down on the larynx.

Many singers lean to one side of that balance. Some have more of the *chiaro*, developing a sharp edge to the sound because it cuts through an orchestra. Although that edge makes the voice audible, the resultant quality is often not very pleasant to hear. Other voices bloom and fill the concert hall, but the hearer can find it difficult to discern the pitch because of a lack of clarity (fundamental tone or core) in the sound. Ideally, we want to balance the *chiaro* and *oscuro*, so the voice cuts through the orchestra but also has the bloom and shimmer to fill a large concert hall. Many singers achieve that, but few do it on a consistent basis throughout their range and repertoire.

A consistent chiaroscuro balance is a difficult technique to acquire. Many musical styles use almost none of the *oscuro* part of the sound, and indeed, it would sound ridiculous to hear country music or hip-hop performed with a fully balanced sound. But once singers have mastered classical chiaroscuro technique and freed their voices, they can choose to form the vowels with less resonance and still sing with a great deal of freedom in any genre. Classical technique is a great foundation for any kind of singing.

The Arpeggio

At first glance, Simply Speaking Simply and Free-Flowing Air appear to be contrasting techniques. However, none of the actions in either Invention excludes the actions of the other. So in the Third Invention, A Balancing Act, we simply do the actions of both at the same time. Done correctly, this exercise achieves both the core and the bloom in the sound, without having to add or manufacture any extra "cut" or richness—it just happens naturally.

This Invention consists of a simple *arpeggio* (broken chord) on the scale degrees 1-3-5-3-1, using the same five vowels we used in Simply Speaking Simply: [ni]-[ne]-[nɑ]-[no]-[nu].

We begin the arpeggio in a low range. With women I usually start around B♭3, A3, or A♭3. With men I usually start around C3 or B♭2, depending on the voice type (with basses I actually start around G2). However, I don't begin in the very lowest part of the range because I want people to start where they comfortably speak. We find the natural speaking range and then sing arpeggios begin-

ni - ne - na - no - nu   ni - ne - na - no - nu

Music Example 6.1. A Balancing Act

ning there so that the clear signal we achieved in Simply Speaking Simply then works with Free-Flowing Air to move through the voice in different ranges.

The arpeggio starts in the natural speaking range on the first note of the triad. As we go up to the third and fifth, we let the air take over. The extent to which the air takes over increases as we move upward in the range. The higher we go, the more it will feel like sighing and releasing the air all the time, whereas in the lower range it feels more like speaking. Every pitch we sing should have the full quality of speaking and sighing, but the sensation of the ratios between the two will change as we move through the range.

To get a true balance in the highest part of the range, the muscles of the vocal folds will vibrate, but because they are stretched long and thin, only a portion of the muscle actually vibrates. The only sensation we have is of air flowing freely through the vocal folds. In the lowest part of the range, we intensify the speaking vibration because the vocal folds are so loose, thick, and relaxed that air is going to flow through without much effort. Speaking maintains a balanced sound in the lower part of the range.

In A Balancing Act, we work mostly in the middle range. I don't push the limits of anyone's range in this Invention because until they have mastered the technique, it is difficult to maintain a balance in the extreme high or low extensions. We start in the speaking range and then skip around at random intervals, just as we did in Simply Speaking Simply, until we have covered the entire middle range.

When women are learning A Balancing Act, I don't take them higher than F5 (or G5 or A♭5 for lighter, higher voices)—in other words, I take them up to what we typically refer to as the top of the *passaggio* (the transition area between the speaking voice and the sighing voice). With men, I don't go higher than E♭4, E4, or F4. The lowest pitch I take women to is A♭3 or A3, and the lowest I go with men is G2.

The key is to make sure that the voice always feels relaxed, with a sensation of constant airflow. Like in Free-Flowing Air, it's not how high you get; it's how you get high that is important. Most men feel very comfortable and relaxed up to around C4 (or closer to B♭3 or A3 for baritones and basses). Up to that point, they don't really have to let the air take over to produce a balanced sound. So we cover the range to about a fifth above this point. The only way to get through the *passaggio* while keeping the cords relaxed is to turn over all effort to the breath. Going a bit past the comfortable range forces us to give in to the air.

The more adept a singer becomes at maintaining a chiaroscuro balance, the more we extend to the extreme high and low parts of the range. But this is not a range extension exercise—its sole purpose is to train the voice to balance the speaking and sighing we learned in the first two Inventions on any pitch. Listen to Audio Sample 9 for examples.

 AUDIO SAMPLE 9: The Arpeggio

VOWEL DEFINITION

Just as in Simply Speaking Simply, vowel definition is an important part of the Third Invention. The middle vowel we sing in the triad is [e], and if we don't use a closed [e] with the base of the tongue back and up, when we move to [ɑ] the tongue muscles will pull down, the air will be diffused, and we won't get any of the bloom we found in the upward sigh. To maintain a consistent airflow, we must sing a closed [e] and then transition into an [ɑ] with the base of the tongue still high and back.

Pure vowel definition is crucial to this exercise because the less entangled our vowels are, the easier it is to get the voice to speak clearly and the air to flow freely throughout the range. As we master this, we can more freely and easily combine the *chiaro* and *oscuro* throughout the range with the utmost beauty and power. Consistent airflow is the key to maintaining a balance, and good vowel definition is the key to consistent airflow.

Legato line is an important part of this. I will discuss this in more detail in chapter 10, but for now suffice it to say that consistent airflow is the basis of legato line, and legato line is what makes A Balancing Act possible.

7

The Fourth Invention: Spontaneous Combustion

Just as in Simply Speaking Simply, the basic neurological impulse to speak is the basis for the action in the Fourth Invention, Spontaneous Combustion. Here we return to basic speech and the original source of utterance, the desire to express and communicate. Spontaneous Combustion happens when we are poised—calm, collected, still, and ready. Spontaneity is not the same as impromptu, which implies a lack of preparation; rather, the spontaneous singer is poised and prepared with the ideal conditions for a spontaneous action to occur. In the same way that poise affects healthy vocalism, it affects performance on stage and in everyday life.

Spontaneous Combustion deals with the beginning of the sound, which is called the *onset*. The traditional term used to describe the beginning of the sound in music is *attack*. I try to avoid using this word because of its violent connotation. The onset of sound is crucial to good singing because the way we produce the sound at the beginning of the phrase has a direct impact on the sound through the rest of the phrase. We must begin singing with the utmost efficiency—the maximum of balanced, full sound with the minimum expenditure of energy—and that is what we learn to do in Spontaneous Combustion.

The philosophical idea behind this Invention is that spontaneity requires vulnerability and openness to the varying circumstances of any given moment. Spontaneity does not mean lack of preparation or readiness; on the contrary, we must be poised and ready for spontaneous, creative action to occur. To perform the actual exercise of Spontaneous Combustion properly, we must be centered and balanced, ready to let go of control and spontaneously go with the flow without anticipating the outcome.

FIVE DETACHED [ɑ]'S

The vocal exercise of Spontaneous Combustion is simple: five detached [ɑ]'s or five onsets on the vowel [ɑ], sung on the same pitch, then repeated randomly throughout the middle range and *passaggio*. Because these sounds are sung on an [ɑ] without a preceding consonant, they are *glottal* onsets (the term *glottal* refers to the glottis, the opening between the vocal folds). Many people suggest that a glottal onset is harmful to the voice, and indeed, the common glottal attack can be damaging. Many singers avoid a glottal attack by aspirating the onset—placing an [h] before the vowel. The aspirated [h] onset begins the sound with airflow and can avoid a harsh coughing-type beginning that is potentially damaging. However, placing an [h] before the vowel separates the vocal folds, which eliminates the possibility of starting immediately with a balanced, chiaroscuro sound.

Once I had the onset in place, all I had to do was to carry through. By talking about the sung lines as lines of speech, of having something to say, I was able to use the air I had and carry the phrase through to the end. Not only does this encompass the realm of communication through the sung line, but it also keeps the singer from building any kind of tension within the musculature of breath or phonation. It does so by encouraging the singer to use the air that is already in the lungs and also shows just how large the true capacity for air is within the lungs.

Teri Herron, soprano

The purpose of this Invention is to learn to phonate so that the entire spectrum of sound is healthily present from the first millisecond. The opposite of this exercise is the style found in most pop and Broadway singing where the singer starts with a straight tone, then adds the vibrato after a few seconds. Some opera singers also start to sing a note without a fully vibrant, balanced sound, then let it bloom. Our goal is to learn to sing with core and bloom, *chiaro* and *oscuro*, from the first moment of phonation. When we begin with balanced phonation, we have a much bet-

MUSIC EXAMPLE 7.1 Spontaneous Combustion

ter chance of carrying through the rest of any sung phrase. The key is to begin correctly.

We do not sustain the sound in this Invention because the specific goal is to have the entire spectrum of the tone (the complete chiaroscuro balance) at the onset. Therefore, there is no advantage to sustaining the tone. We sing five short, detached [ɑ]'s.

The number five is somewhat arbitrary, except as a way to get a sense of rhythm in the exercise—singing four notes and ending on a downbeat. However, doing five (as opposed to four or six) onsets is not crucial. If it becomes too rhythmic, singers can easily lose the sense of spontaneity, which negates the purpose. Repeating the [ɑ] five times requires us to keep the sound fresh and new, and we can perfect the production of the vowel on each repetition. If the first onset [ɑ] feels tight and flat, we define the [ɑ] to disentangle the articulators from the phonation.

We begin the five detached [ɑ]'s in the middle range. With women I begin around Ab4 or A4; with tenors I begin around A3, with baritones around Ab3, and with basses around G3 or F♯3. In the beginning stages of this exercise, I stay in the middle of the voice, and even with advanced singers, I typically cover only about an octave (extending a fourth or fifth above and below the beginning note). As people get better at doing this exercise, we can extend the range somewhat, but in the beginning we stay generally within an octave.

This is not a range extension exercise; its purpose is to achieve a balanced sound from the first moment of phonation. Just as we did in Simply Speaking Simply, we phonate with a clean, clear signal; however, Spontaneous Combustion is a more refined Invention because we speak with the articulators completely out of the way (i.e., the tongue up and back, the soft palate raised, and the jaw dropped to the [ɑ] position). When we phonate with the articulators out of the way, we can get a complete chiaroscuro sound. Otherwise, the voice can become entangled and the tone imbalanced. Listen to Audio Sample 10 for examples.

AUDIO SAMPLE 10: Detached [ɑ]'s

I use [ɑ] in all of the Inventions:

- In Simply Speaking Simply, we say [ni]-[ne]-[nɑ]-[no]-[nu].
- In Free-Flowing Air we begin with [ɑ] and modulate to [o] as we ascend.
- In A Balancing Act, we again sing [ni]-[ne]-[nɑ]-[no]-[nu], with [ɑ] in the center.
- Spontaneous Combustion and The Wobble both use [ɑ] exclusively.
- Getting High uses [e]-[ɑ]-[o].

My approach to singing is based on [ɑ], and the reason I use it so much is that [ɑ] is the only vowel that cannot be set or held and still sound like [ɑ]. We can set or tighten either of the tongue vowels [i] or [e] and they still sound like [i] and [e] only tighter. Likewise, if we sing [o] and [u], and then set or tighten the articulators, they still sound like [o] and [u].

However, if we say [ɑ] and set or tighten the articulators, it will no longer sound like [ɑ]. Thus, [ɑ]—more than any other vowel—must be mentally rather than physically defined for it to be free. A correctly defined [ɑ] is crucial for all of the Inventions, but particularly so in Spontaneous Combustion

The breakthrough moment for me was the day I realized my own [ɑ] vowel sufficed sans tongue color or jaw tension. It's invigorating to sing my own [ɑ] vowel without any added "mezzo" ingredients.

Sasha Cooke, mezzo-soprano

because making a balanced chiaroscuro sound from the first moment requires freedom. Likewise, we can only sing a correct [ɑ] vowel if the voice is truly free, so there is no margin of error in this exercise: We either do it correctly and get a balanced sound or we do it incorrectly and get an imbalanced sound. Listen to Audio Sample 11 for an example.

 AUDIO SAMPLE 11: [ɑ] Sung Correctly and Incorrectly

Poise is the key to this Invention. To be poised means that the voice is prepared to make a fully balanced sound immediately. In technical terms, *poise* means the body is poised to respond and the articulators are up, back and away from the vocal folds themselves, so that they do not entangle the vocal folds'

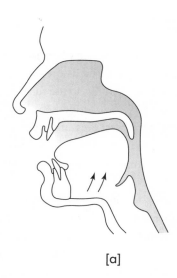

[ɑ]

FIGURE 7.1. Tongue and soft palate in correct [ɑ] position

vibration. To do this, I have singers visualize the [ɑ] vowel with the soft palate lifted and the back of the tongue raised high (see Figure 7.1). This separates
the articulators from the actual vibration of the vocal folds, and the distance
between the two allows the larynx to speak the five detached [ɑ]'s, free from
supraglottal entanglement. Also, when we speak, we don't close the glottis with
any subglottal pressure. So, when Spontaneous Combustion is done correctly,
we make a balanced chiaroscuro sound free from both subglottal and supraglottal entanglements.

Once we have visualized the [ɑ] and raised the articulators up and out of
the way, we spontaneously speak so that the only movement is in the larynx. If
we do this correctly, the body will respond to this spontaneous phonation with
air. We don't think about airflow when doing the detached [ɑ]'s—but if the
body is poised, the air is responsive to the spontaneous speaking.

We refine the clean, clear signal we achieved in Simply Speaking Simply.
The difference is that in that Invention we were not trying to get a balanced
sound; rather, we were focused on the *chiaro*, core or bright part of the sound.
In Spontaneous Combustion, we take that clarity a step further and, through
the definition of [ɑ], the *oscuro* resonance is added. As we phonate freely and
keep the articulators free from the action of the vocal folds, the sound will be
balanced—we will always have both *chiaro* and *oscuro* in the sound.

Physiologically, when we do this Invention correctly, the two sides of the glottis touch, vibrate, and then open again. That is the only activity that should happen once we have visualized the [ɑ]. I like to use the word *touch* to describe that activity because very often people overadduct the vocal folds to feel the closure of the glottis, which creates subglottal pressure and inhibits airflow. To think of the vocal folds touching suggests an unforced, relaxed action that occurs naturally, almost involuntarily, when we want to express something through talking or singing.

We want the vocal folds to touch to get a clear onset. However, we must not press the folds together, causing a cough-like onset with a lot of subglottal pressure. We also don't want to start with any aspiration because if we put an [h] before the vowel, the vocal folds are not touching. In Spontaneous Combustion, we want to find a balance between the pressed onset and the aspirated onset. There should be no sensation of subglottal pressure, and when it is right, we don't really feel the glottis closing.

The only way to begin with a clear onset is to think that we are about to speak. When we prepare to speak, the vocal cords close easily on their own. If we force the glottis closed, the air can't flow in or out, and we don't want that feeling in Spontaneous Combustion. We do use a glottal onset, but it is not hard on the voice, and in fact it is very healthy for the voice to speak without any pressure.

A PRACTICAL TOOL

In addition to being a tool for learning a healthy onset, Spontaneous Combustion serves a variety of other purposes.

First, if we have no subglottal pressure and our vowels are defined so that the articulators are up and away from the vocal folds, we become very sensitive to any subglottal pressure. We feel the pressure immediately. As soon as we feel any subglottal pressure, we are able to alleviate it.

Second, this Invention is useful when working through repertoire. If we are singing along in a piece and come across a note that doesn't speak or resonate freely, we can detach the vowel on that note. As we vocalize the onset on that note repeatedly, we get the feeling that the vocal cords are clear and free from pressure and we also get a sense of the balance and resonance that we should feel when singing that note in context. Once we have sung the vowel alone and detached, we put the correct consonants in front of it and sing the detached vowel with consonants. Once again, we must beware that the consonant doesn't grab the cords or force them closed.

Third, this Invention is useful in learning how to sing *staccato*. *Staccato* literally means "detached." Coloratura sopranos have to master this technique to sing the staccato passages, as in the Queen of the Night's aria in Mozart's opera *The Magic Flute*, as well as many other *bel canto* standards. Two common approaches to these passages include using an aspirated detachment or a forced glottal cutoff, which causes the next note to begin with an abusive glottal "attack" and prohibits airflow (more on this topic in chapter 10).

By mastering the detached vowel onset, we can sing detached vowels clearly with a consonant-like glottal onset. For example, if we just speak the line: [tɑ]-[tɑ]-[tɑ]-[tɑ]-[tɑ], the nonvoiced consonant [t] is stopping the phonation, but it feels like the air is still flowing steadily throughout the phrase. The flow of air retains a legato feel. Similarly, if we think of the glottal onset as being like a consonant, we don't need to cut off the first note with a glottal stop; we simply begin the second note with a glottal onset. Because the glottal onset is a momentary stop of the phonation, we will get a detached sound, but in a healthy way. Listen to Audio Sample 12 for an example.

 AUDIO SAMPLE 12: Detached [ɑ]'s and Forced Glottal Closure [ɑ]'s

THE RELEASE

Spontaneous Combustion is primarily about mastering the onset, but a secondary consideration is mastering the release. In the onset, the cords simply touch and vibrate. To release (or stop) the sound, the cords just open, and that simple opening should be the only kind of release. The common term for the release is *cutoff*, but again, I don't like that term because of its violent connotations. People literally cut off the sound by squeezing the cords tighter and stopping the breath. This can be just as abusive as forcing the cords closed in the glottal attack.

We get a healthy release by inhaling to stop phonation. If the vocal cords are vibrating and we simply inhale, the cords will open easily and naturally, without a forced cutoff. The challenge of using inhalation as the release is that breathing in becomes a reaction to what we have just done (phonation), and all inhalation should be a preparation for the next word, phrase, or note.

So to make the release free without contaminating the preparation of the next phrase, I teach a release of phonation while the air continues to flow. This is accomplished by attempting a quick decrescendo. In this kind of decrescendo, the vocal folds gradually abduct, and the sound diffuses. There is no strain on the vocal folds in this kind of release, yet because the air is still flowing after the vibration of the vocal folds has ceased, the singer is free to inhale as preparation for the next phrase or pitch. As this is perfected in Spontaneous Combustion, there is no entanglement or movement in the base of the tongue during the onset or release of the sound.

The Fifth Invention: The Wobble

Why would any singer want to master the art of the wobble? A wobble is usually associated with the elderly soprano in the church choir whose vibrato is big enough to drive a truck through. No singer wants a wobble, and no audience wants to hear a voice wobbling out of control. So why in the world would I use this word? There is a simple reason: I call it The Wobble for its shock effect. It tends to stir people up and get them thinking about vocal control in a different way.

Of all the Inventions, The Wobble is the only one that I may have invented entirely myself. It came to me when I was trying to teach a singer to stop controlling his voice and submit completely to the airflow, which is the intention of this exercise. When we give up control of the larynx, singing various intervals will feel like an out-of-control wobble, so using that term helps conceptualize the sensation of total loss of control, which is, in fact, true freedom.

Flexibility is the key positive concept of this Invention. Flexibility (emotional, vocal, and psychological) requires vulnerability, and The Wobble is impossible to do if a singer is not flexible and vulnerable. Mastering The Wobble adds flexibility to the clean articulation, airflow, evenness, and strength gained in the first four inventions. It also enhances the ability to use airflow to move freely through the middle passage to the top of the voice.

MUSIC EXAMPLE 8.1. The Wobble

The application of The Wobble is simple. We just alternate between pitches that are four tones apart, first slowly and then quickly. We begin singing [ɑ] on a given pitch and then sing another [ɑ] up a fourth from the first pitch, and then alternate those pitches for four quarter notes, followed by two beats of eight sixteenth notes (also on [ɑ]), ending with a quarter note [ɑ] on the original pitch.

After one round of the exercise, we move up a half step and reverse the exercise to alternate from high to low. If we begin on the low pitch, we end on the low pitch; likewise, if we begin on the high pitch, we end on the high pitch. We alternate beginning on high and low pitches every other time because it helps us avoid getting stuck in a pattern that sets the vocal cords in a predictable position.

Obviously the "wobble" part of the Invention is the sixteenth notes, where we are wobbling the voice back and forth quickly between those pitches. The first four quarter notes simply establish the pitch. But the voice must be loose and free with the air flowing freely to sing the sixteenth notes correctly—or to wobble correctly.

The Wobble begins in the low part of the range. With women, I usually start somewhere around B♭3, A3, or A♭3. With men, the beginning pitch, again, has a wider variation. With tenors I begin around C3 or C♯3, with baritones around a B2, B♭2, or A2; with basses I usually begin around A♭2, G2, or sometimes as low as F2. Please refer to Audio Sample 13 for examples.

 AUDIO SAMPLE 13: The Wobble

THE FOURTH INTERVAL

The purpose of The Wobble is to develop flexibility with airflow. We use an interval of a fourth because with smaller intervals it is possible to hold the voice and still hit the notes. But when we go as wide as a fourth, it is almost impos-

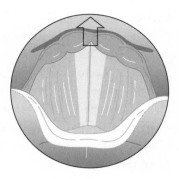

FIGURE 8.1. Vocal folds stretch longer and thinner for higher pitches

sible to hold the voice in a position and still sing the pitches. The only way to successfully do The Wobble is to loosen the vocal folds and let them stretch back and forth freely for the various pitches.

Physiologically speaking, The Wobble stretches the vocal folds long and thin and then releases them to become short and thick in quick succession. The vocal folds are attached at opposite ends to two different cartilage structures, which rock back and forth in relation to each other as the folds stretch and relax. Allowing these cartilages to rock in this fashion feels like giving up control of the voice, literally allowing it to wobble. When the folds phonate the lower pitch of the fourth interval, they are shorter, thicker and more relaxed. When we move to the higher pitch, the vocal folds stretch longer, tighter and thinner (see Figure 8.1).

Often when singers move back and forth quickly on various pitches, they tend to squeeze the adductor muscles tighter, which pinches the cords and resists airflow. Instead of sounding like two pitches sung freely, this squeezing action creates a sound like a car motor trying to start with a low battery, with an uneven and forced fluctuation between pitches. That is why we must do The Wobble in a strict rhythm, particularly the sixteenth notes. Singing those notes with an even rhythm encourages the air to flow steadily without pinching the cords together on the high note. Pinched cords invariably interrupt the rhythm because when they are tight, we have to use subglottal pressure to force the air through. Without total flexibility and freedom in the cords, we get a surge of air every time we try to sing high, and the rhythm becomes uneven.

The goal in The Wobble (and in singing generally) is to have air flowing through the vocal folds steadily and freely throughout the range. In the Fourth Invention, Spontaneous Combustion, phonation is active and airflow is passive. In The Wobble, airflow is active and phonation is passive. However, both, if done correctly, will produce a balanced chiaroscuro sound.

To keep the air flowing freely in The Wobble, we must keep the vocal folds as relaxed and loose as possible. Of course, when we sing higher pitches, the cords do stretch longer and tighter, but that is different than squeezing. If we don't tighten the adductor muscles, the arytenoids will be no closer together on a high pitch than they are on a low pitch, and the air can flow in a steady stream from high to low. It is crucial that we feel like phonation is passive by keeping the vocal cords loose, thus allowing air to flow through steadily as they lengthen and shorten.

SINGING FIORATURA PASSAGES

The Wobble is the key Invention for gaining the flexibility necessary to sing *fioratura* passages (musical sections that use rapid pitches in scales or broken chords). There is a common perception that big voices just can't sing *fioratura*, but I disagree. Every voice, no matter its size, should be able to do *fioratura* because when the voice is truly free, we can sing any number of pitches at any speed. Of course, we expect coloratura sopranos to be able to negotiate these passages, but all voices should be able to sing *fioratura*, and indeed most voices are required at some point to do so, especially in music by Handel, Bach, Mozart, and any of the *bel canto* composers (more about singing *fioratura* in Chapter 10).

The Wobble also helps people let go of vocal, emotional, and psychological control, letting the air carry the sound and be a source of power for the voice. Giving up control is extremely difficult, which is why I use the word *wobble*— it forces people to think differently about how they use their voice, and the extreme connotation of the word takes people further down the path to letting go of control than they might otherwise be willing to go. This is also why I use terms like *flabby* and *flexible* to emphasize the need to give up control and allow the voice to create the sensation of a wobble when singing any interval in any range of the voice.

9

The Sixth Invention: Getting High

The Sixth Invention, Getting High, is a synthesis of all of the previous exercises and a further refinement of the skills acquired. It assumes a high level of clean phonation, free-flowing air, tonal balance, spontaneity, and flexibility. Technically, it involves a lengthy scale that begins in the lowest part of the voice and modulates as it moves upward and then returns to the low voice. Philosophically, Getting High involves stretching and reaching for our fullest potential, pushing beyond what is comfortable and easy. On one level, Getting High refers to the euphoria of transcending limitations, enhancing abilities, and broadening horizons. On another level, this invention is about extending our vocal range—literally *getting high*.

There is a symmetry to the six Inventions. In the first, Simply Speaking Simply, we focus on speaking, and we swing the pendulum fully to the *chiaro* side of the sound spectrum. In the second, Free-Flowing Air, we focus on airflow and swing the pendulum to the opposite, *oscuro* side of the spectrum. In the third, A Balancing Act, we combine the first two to find a balanced chiaroscuro sound in the middle. In the fourth, Spontaneous Combustion, we return our focus to the *chiaro* at a refined level, then back to a refined *oscuro* in The Wobble. In the final Invention, we return once again to the balanced middle,

MUSIC EXAMPLE 9.1. Getting High

employing the techniques of clear phonation, free-flowing air, chiaroscuro balance, clean onset/release, and flexibility throughout the vocal range.

The goal in Getting High is to train the voice to naturally and instinctively modulate between the extremes of *chiaro* and *oscuro*. As the voice ascends and descends in a scale, it will not be balanced in the sense that we will have equal amounts of phonation and airflow all the time. The *sound* will always be balanced, but the *sensation* we experience is that the ratio of phonation to airflow will shift as we move through the range. In the lower part of the range, the ratio will lean toward speaking; in the upper range, it will lean much more toward airflow.

The exercise for Getting High is an eleven-tone scale sung on seventeen notes. We begin on a pitch in the lower part of the range and ascend on a major scale eleven notes (to the fourth scale degree in the second octave). Then we descend on a dominant seventh chord, arriving finally on the original pitch where we began.

We use specific vowels when singing the scale, beginning on a closed [e] for four notes; then we shift to [ɑ] for four notes, then to [o] for the duration of the scale. I chose those vowels specifically to encourage the voice to shift and modulate from a more *speaking* sensation in the lower part of the voice to a *sigh* or airflow sensation in the upper range of the voice. In a way, this is a refinement of the siren phase of Free-Flowing Air because the air must flow just as consistently from top to bottom in both exercises; the difference in Getting High is that we are now specifying and fully phonating all of the notes. But the transition from [ɑ] to [o] (i.e., only rounding the lips to an [o]) in the siren should be exactly the same as in Getting High so that the articulators allow the air to continually flow freely into the highest range of the voice. That shift is what lets the air take over as we go up.

The two qualities of speaking and sighing should be present to some degree on every pitch, but the sensation of speaking in the lower range will always be much greater than it is in the high range. As we go to the top, the sensation of sigh in the sound will be much greater than the sensation of speaking. Getting High allows that shift to happen naturally, without manipulating the vocal folds, the tongue, or the jaw to make it happen.

AUTOMATIC TRANSMISSION

I often use an analogy of automatic transmission versus manual transmission to help explain the process of "shifting gears" in Getting High. After moving to New York, I came across students who didn't drive, so I have almost completely stopped using this analogy. But for those who drive or have driven cars it is still a valuable way to understand the process, so I have decided to include it here.

At an early age, I learned to drive both manual and automatic transmission vehicles, and when I learned to sing, I found an interesting comparison between good singing and driving with automatic transmission. When we sing, the amount of speaking and airflow in the sound is shifting constantly. Every time we change a vowel, a pitch, a dynamic level, or an emotional intent, the resonance shifts. Those shifts should happen naturally and smoothly, just as a car with automatic transmission shifts effortlessly from first through fifth gear (or higher).

Our goal is to sing like a Lexus with automatic transmission, shifting through the vocal registers with imperceptible precision. When driving an expensive, well-made car, we don't even think about shifting gears—we just drive. Likewise, in singing we should not notice when modulating between ratios of speaking and airflow or from low to high—we should just sing and let the changes happen smoothly and effortlessly on their own.

MIXING CHEST AND HEAD VOICE

A common way people discuss this shift is "mixing head voice and chest voice." I tend to avoid that terminology because it generally causes people to think about how it feels when shifting from head voice to chest voice. They try to manufacture that feeling rather than just letting it happen naturally. When we sing with "automatic transmission," we just phonate and let the air flow freely. The sensation is that it shifts as we sing higher, but we don't *make* it shift. We should never sing like a manual transmission, consciously thinking, "I will now shift into a medium mix between speaking and airflow, then at a certain point I will shift to a higher head voice mix." We simply allow ourselves to let the voice shift naturally on its own, without making it do anything.

Most singers, even some with a lot of training, sing as though they were a two-speed manual transmission car. Though it is actually possible to, say, drive from New York to California using only two speeds, it is certainly *not* the most efficient way to get there, and it will eventually wear out your car. If, for example, you use only first and third gear, you can actually make it across the country, but when you get on the freeway and try to drive at high speeds in third gear, you will strain the motor and possibly throw a rod. Also, if you want to drive at twenty or twenty-five miles per hour without second gear, you'll either be racing in first gear or have very little power in third.

Likewise, the voice has to be in the right "gear" to have power and freedom throughout the range. Broadway belters are classic examples of driving across the country in first gear or all chest voice. They have power and strength as long as they are singing low, but when they get to the top of where first gear can take them, they start to strain and eventually they might "throw a rod," or develop vocal fold problems. So when they begin to feel that strain, they usually shift up to fourth or fifth gear, into a very heady, fluty sound that feels totally disconnected from the voice. This creates a rather obvious break between the head voice and chest voice.

Classical singers often try to mix chest voice and head voice, but that effort often creates a manipulated sound that is strong in neither the low nor the high range. The middle range of the voice is where we develop vocal strength, but trying to "mix" the registers there often weakens this range. The sensation we are going for is something completely new and fresh every time we sing. We should always let the voice shift freely, without being conscious of what "gear" we are in. It will simply be strong on every pitch. A common problem with classically trained women, especially sopranos, is that they have learned to sing always in head voice and they are afraid to use chest voice in the lower range. Their low voices sound very weak and imbalanced because they don't let the "low gears" function. That is the opposite of Broadway belters or country singers who never use the head voice or sing in their upper registers but stay in first or second gear all the time.

The transmission analogy eventually breaks down because the human voice is a much more complex instrument than a car motor. Most cars have only four or five gears, but the human voice actually has hundreds of gears. We change gears every half step because every note in the range will have a different ratio of speaking to airflow. Also, every time we change a vowel, an emotional intent, or a dynamic level, the note will resonate differently, so we might even shift gears on the same note. So there are literally hundreds of shifts that take place throughout our range.

The eleven-tone scale in Getting High actually trains us to loosen the vocal folds and let the shifts and adjustments happen naturally and easily by using the vowels [e]-[ɑ]-[o]. This vowel progression moves from [e] which more easily "speaks" to [o], which has much more natural back space and encourages airflow—simply by its articulation. It would seem logical, then, to assume that we should "downshift" to [ɑ] and then [e] as we descend. However, we stay on [o] because when singers descend, they often let up on the airflow, and [o] encourages airflow all the way back down to the low voice.

START LOW

We begin the scale in the lower range, in approximately the same range where we begin The Wobble. For women, that is around B♭3, A3, or A♭3; tenors begin around a C3, baritones around B♭2 or A2, and basses at A♭2, G2, or F♯2. We begin on a closed [e] for four notes, then shift to [ɑ] for four notes then to [o] for the final three notes of the ascent, then stay on [o] through the descending dominant seventh chord to the final note. The tongue is the only thing that should move as we shift from [e] to [ɑ]. The arch of the tongue in [e] will flatten slightly as we shift to [ɑ], but the jaw and the lips should not move at all. The visible part of the tongue will be slightly flatter, but the back of the tongue and the soft palate remain high for both [e] and [ɑ]. Then when we shift to [o], the only change in the articulators is a rounding of the lips, which encourages airflow. We repeat the scale, moving up by half steps, extending the voice into the highest possible pitch. When we reach a point where we can no longer sing through the scale in full voice, we shift to falsetto, or pure head voice.

Women can typically sing this scale in full voice up to A5 or B♭5 with freedom and ease. But when they get to B5 or C6 they don't want to fully release their voice as much as is necessary to shift into what I call "flute" voice because it sounds very airy and fluty and feels "off the voice." This is different from whistle tone, which is actually one "gear shift" above flute voice. In flute voice, women usually feel less engaged, but they still produce a full-voiced sound despite it being almost all airflow. If women manage to release the vocal folds into flute voice, it extends their range up to E♭6 or E6. Most women I teach can sing as high as E♭6 or E6, but not much higher. There are some women who can sing higher, but it requires a shift into the "whistle voice" register. The difference with whistle voice is that because the cords are so much longer, thinner, and tighter and a much smaller portion of the cords is actually vibrating, it feels like a whistle sound without any tone at all. I work hard to get all of my female students to find flute voice, but usually only the lighter, smaller, coloratura voices ever discover the whistle voice register. Of course, some of the fuller-voiced women do access the whistle voice, but it's not common and certainly not necessary.

Every gear has the potential of all the other gears if we truly sing freely. The more gears we can discover, the more potential freedom we have in the voice.

So there is some value in extending a woman's range all the way up into the whistle voice.

Male singers experience a different phenomenon. Men have to give over completely to the sensation of airflow at what is called the *secondo passaggio*, or the top of the transitional passage from chest voice to head voice. However, the key to singing through and above the *passaggio* is to give over to the air before the *primo passaggio*, or the bottom of the transitional passage, which is usually around middle C for tenors or slightly lower than that for lower male voices. When men shift into head voice or the upper register and give in to the airflow, their full voices can extend up to about B♭4 for tenors and slightly lower for baritones and basses. Most tenors should shift around B♭4, but they often just push through it, using the same sensation on B♭4 as on B4 and C5, so C5 becomes the highest note they can sing. What should happen is another shift to pure falsetto, which enables the voice to sing up to F5 or higher.

We learn to let those shifts happen naturally, not at specific points in the range, but by constant, individual shifts on each note. When we achieve a natural and free "automatic transmission" sensation, the listener will not hear a shift as we move through the vocal range. As men shift into falsetto, the B and C will sound vital, with a lot of vibration and ring, but it will feel very much like pure falsetto. That can only happen if we gradually shift all the way to the top.

At some point, I always tell men to let the voice shift into falsetto. In the early stages, the shift will be very obvious—I hear a crack or a bump as they shift from full-voice to falsetto. As we progress, we work on blurring the line between falsetto and full voice by making it so the muscle gradually goes out of the vocalism as airflow takes over, but the shift is imperceptible. When the voice is truly free and loose, it will feel like it is shifting all the time, on every pitch—not that we are making it shift, but that we are allowing those shifts to happen naturally as a result of proper conditioning. As we master this technique, our vocal range will continue to expand, as will our ability to sing difficult vocal repertoire.

I teach a few male singers who, because of their youth and a naturally free falsetto, are able to sing up to F6. That is not necessary or common; however, most men can eventually get as high as F5. Some can go higher, but I don't believe there is much value in continuing to stretch beyond that for all voices. I do believe in stretching the limit of each individual voice to its highest potential. Some of the best low basses can sing up to the F5 or F♯5 because they have worked on it so long and diligently and have established a great deal of freedom and looseness in the voice. However, I do not push people in the early stages to sing beyond what feels comfortable because, just as in Free-Flowing Air, it's not how high you get, it's how you get high that is important. Please refer to Audio Sample 14 for examples.

 AUDIO SAMPLE 14: The Eleven-Tone Scale

When we have mastered the eleven-tone scale of Getting High, the voice will shift naturally throughout the range, we will have freedom in singing higher pitches, and we get to the point where we feel we have reached the limit of our physical capabilities. The euphoria of reaching that point creates a sense of emotional and mental freedom—we no longer have to worry about singing high notes because we know that they will be there for us as we sing freely and healthily throughout the range. We let the voice shift constantly, blurring the lines between full voice and falsetto and eventually develop what I would call *perfect technique*.

PERFECT TECHNIQUE

Perfect technique, in my opinion, is the ability to sing from a pure falsetto to a full-voiced, ringing, balanced sound on any pitch and on any vowel without feeling or hearing where the shift between the two happens. This is called *messa di voce*, going from the softest pianissimo to the loudest forte and back again without any trace of a register shift.

Messa di voce is almost impossible without complete freedom and flexibility in the voice, and I've heard no singer in the world who does it perfectly on every pitch and vowel throughout the range. When I demonstrate the *messa di voce* technique to students, I usually tell them, "Don't try this at home!" because until they have developed all of the techniques in the Inventions, they will become frustrated when trying to achieve it. Mastering the Inventions will eventually give people the power, freedom, and flexibility to do a *messa di voce* throughout the range but will also condition them for the real job of singing— "where the rubber meets the road."

Part

III

WHERE THE RUBBER MEETS THE ROAD

Playing the Game

The skills and techniques we gained in the Inventions are crucial to conditioning and training the voice, but conditioning is very different from singing repertoire (any piece of music). Many additional factors come into play once we begin applying technique to repertoire. The Inventions are designed to be an exercise routine that conditions us to "play the game," but it is not the same as actually performing. Singing a piece of music is "playing the game."

For example, athletes train constantly for years to gain the strength, agility, speed, and endurance necessary to compete in the Olympic Games. Their training includes a very specific exercise routine that contains elements of their sport. They also have tests and trials in their specific events. However, doing those exercises is a very different experience from actually competing in the Olympics. Playing the game involves being spontaneous, making quick decisions, and having enough clarity of mind to strategize under pressure while utilizing the skills and conditioning gained in the regular exercise routine.

Similarly, singers should not be thinking about technique when singing a piece of music. We apply our skills and techniques while learning repertoire so that we don't have to think about those things when singing. This chapter attempts to address some of the most common additional skills and challenges involved in singing (or "playing the game").

In the introduction to the Inventions, I defined *legato* as a smooth, even style without any noticeable break between the notes. Creating a constant balance of phonation and airflow with consistent intensity is what I call legato technique. When we begin applying technique to repertoire, legato is the overriding principle that guides our choices as we negotiate difficult or challenging passages. Many musical styles don't require the legato technique needed for classical music; however, learning to sing with legato technique is the basis for healthy singing in any style.

> Learning how to use my voice with less tension and pressure enables me to sing many different styles (i.e., jazz, classical, folk, etc.) and in many ranges of my voice with ease and vocal health.
>
> Aric Schneller, tenor

Vowel Definition

The most important consideration in legato technique is vowel definition. As we discussed throughout the Inventions, the two basic actions of singing are phonation and airflow. These actions are simple enough. Complications arise when we begin to sing vowels in addition to those we defined in the Inventions. Learning to articulate the vowels while maintaining free phonation and airflow is the first and most important step in applying technique to repertoire. We must learn to define each vowel specifically to ensure the utmost freedom of the voice. Vowels are defined by moving the articulators (lips, tongue, jaw, and soft palate). The way we move the articulators directs the airflow. I call this "channeling the air." We channel the air by defining the vowels so that the air seems to continually flow through the vowel along the "sigh" path.

A vowel is a sound that has no interruption of the airflow. In singing repertoire, we are using words. Words contain a combination of vowels and consonants. Typically, when singing in our native language, we pay less attention to defining vowels because we assume we know the correct way to articulate them. But native speakers of any language must learn to channel their air through refined vowel definition. We want to have no sensation of resistance to the airflow and no entanglement of phonation while singing any vowel on any pitch. How we move our articulators to define those vowels is a crucial part of singing.

In the Inventions we learned how to freely and clearly articulate the five Italian vowels [i]-[e]-[ɑ]-[o]-[u]. How we define those vowels channels the air into the sigh space we accessed in Free-Flowing Air. The key to defining any vowel beyond those five Italian vowels, then, is to learn to articulate them in a way that will enable us to sigh them or let the air flow freely through them along the sigh path. One way to do this is to speak the entire text of a song or an aria in a sigh-like falsetto. Whether sung on pitch or not, this trains us to let air flow freely through every syllable of every word. Poor articulation of the vowels can diminish or completely interrupt the airflow, so we have to find a way to articulate the vowel so that the air can continue to flow.

I should mention here that I take issue with the concept of "vowel modification" as it is normally taught. This common practice means that when we get to the upper limits of our vocal range and the voice starts to get tight, we change the vowel to release tension. Singers are often taught to "cover" the vowel, so a pure [i] becomes [ɪ] as in "sit," [e] becomes [ɛ] as in "set" or even [ɑ]. These modifications can make the voice feel less tense, but by singing a completely different vowel we corrupt the integrity of the expression. There is a big difference in meaning between the words *seen* and *sin*, and *late*, *let*, and *lot*, yet singers often change vowels this drastically. We should maintain the integrity of the vowels no matter how high or low we sing, and we do that by defining them so that they sound like the original vowel without interrupting the airflow.

The dilemma is that most people assume they have to define vowels in singing just as they do in speech. That is an incorrect assumption. An [i] can still sound exactly like a pure [i] in the highest range of the voice, but the articulation of that [i] will feel very different from regular speech (refer back to Figure 4.2). The singer's job is to learn how to sing the [i] freely throughout the upper range and not morph every vowel into [ɑ]. It is a cop-out to change vowels in the top of the voice. Doing so may feel free, but it lacks integrity and indicates a faulty technique.

The solution is to articulate each vowel so that the air flows freely and phonation is disentangled. When we are able to do that, we can sing every vowel in its pure form, even though it may feel different from regular speech.

The [i] is a great example because it is indigenous to almost every language. When we articulate an [i] normally, the tongue is thrust forward in the mouth, the tip of the tongue touches the back of the lower teeth, and the arch of the tongue touches and extends outside the upper molars. I have discovered that what really defines the [i] is the arch of the tongue touching the upper molars. The [i] is not defined by the specific *place* at which the arch of the tongue touches the molars. Also, a pure [i] *can* be produced without the tip of the tongue touching the back of the lower teeth.

As I worked to maintain the integrity of [i] in the top of my voice, I discovered that if I held on to the same [i] position that I use in everyday speech, my voice tightened and I couldn't sing a pure [i] up high. However, if I relaxed and dropped my jaw as if to say [ɑ] and then, without moving my jaw, sang a pure [i], I still got the sound of [i]. But my tongue was in a very different position from how I said [i] in everyday speech. In fact, my tongue touched the molars much farther back than with the [i] in everyday speech. It felt much different from everyday speech, but I could sing a pure [i] in that articulation and still maintain a loose larynx and free-flowing air. I realized that I should sing all of my [i]'s with that articulation, no matter what range I was singing. So if we understand what is essential to make each vowel sound, we can maintain that part of articulation while keeping the jaw dropped in an [ɑ] position.

I also discovered that moving the jaw is not necessary to sing any vowel in any language. That does not mean the jaw should be locked in position; rather, the only time the jaw must move is when articulating certain consonants. I do not mean every vowel should sound like [ɑ]; on the contrary, every vowel should be distinct and pure. This just means that movement of the jaw away from the [ɑ] position is not a necessary part of any vowel definition. We commonly move the jaw in conjunction with moving the lips or the tongue, but that is not necessary.

Much of our work in vowel definition deals with getting the articulators to move independently of each other. We can train the jaw and the tongue to function separately—what I call separation of function. The jaw should always feel unhinged. That does not mean that we drop the jaw so far that it becomes tight. It means that the muscle that controls the hinge allows the jaw to open as far as it can without becoming tight. When we bite down and grit our teeth, this muscle protrudes at the sides of the jaw. This is the masseter muscle, and it should always remain relaxed and free during singing. (Refer back to Figure 4.6.) This can happen while singing any vowel. The tongue and the lips have separate functions from the jaw, and we must train ourselves to use them separately. The goal is to use the lips and the tongue to channel the air along the sigh path without tension in the jaw.

I should also mention the function of the soft palate. It is difficult to get the soft palate to move independently of airflow. Some people can lift their soft palate independently, but I find that this happens automatically with the correct channeling of the air, so it is not something we need to focus on. Often people are told to breathe into a yawn position before singing. That does raise the soft palate, but it also depresses the back of the tongue. A more correct idea is to breathe into the "upper half" of the yawn without pressing down on the back of the tongue. If the air is flowing and the lips and tongue define the vowels without entangling the larynx, then the soft palate will lift in response. Lifting the soft palate is not something we necessarily need to do. It happens on its own under the right conditions.

Vowel Substitution

Sometimes we *must* substitute a different vowel to maintain balance and air-flow, which is what some people mean in using the idea of vowel modification. I call this "vowel substitution." With this idea, we find a vowel that when sung sounds authentic but allows for free-flowing air. For example, a sound that happens about every fourth syllable in English is "uh." We use it in both the stressed [ʌ] and unstressed [ə] form. The problem with this sound is that the quality is always flat and spread. To keep the quality vibrant and the air flowing freely to a payoff resonance space, we should substitute [ɑ] for this sound.

Another problematic vowel in English is [æ] as in "cat." In the spoken form of [æ], the base of the tongue presses forward and spreads wide, and the soft palate flattens. Therefore the quality becomes strident. So I recommend imagining an [ɑ] vowel to keep the soft palate high and the tongue narrow, and then allowing the base of the tongue to only slightly move forward to give the sound of [æ]. The goal is to choose a vowel that will sound authentic but remains vocally balanced and free. Listen to Audio Samples 15 and 16 for examples.

AUDIO SAMPLE 15: (Singing "The Love of Fudge") Converting Accented [ʌ] and Unaccented [ə] to [ɑ]

AUDIO SAMPLE 16: (Singing "Drat that Cat") Keeping [æ] Vertical

I want to comment specifically on the four French nasal vowels. The amount of nasality in the four French vowels is slight, and English-speaking students often go too far to make them sound nasal. Even the IPA symbols for these vowels, I feel, are misleading, because if we are going to sing them without excessive nasality, we actually substitute a different vowel than is represented by the symbol.

The Four French Nasal Vowels, [œ̃] [ɑ̃] [ɛ̃] [õ]

The [œ̃] comes closest to correctly representing the actual vowel we sing. We just articulate it by forming an [ɛ] with the tongue (as discussed in Simply Speaking Simply), then round the lips to an [ɔ] and add a slight nasal quality. The sung [ɑ̃] is much closer to the [ɔ] as in "haughty" than a regular [ɑ], and then we use almost no nasality. The sung [ɛ̃] is defined much more like the

English [æ], as in "cat," with very little nasality. The [ō] should just be sung closed with slight nasality. Listen to Audio Sample 17 for examples.

 AUDIO SAMPLE 17: French Nasal Vowels

Consonants

As I said before, a vowel is a sound that has no interruption of the airflow. A consonant, however, is a partial or complete interruption of the airflow. Consonants are essential to understanding text, so our goal is to learn how to articulate consonants clearly with minimal interruption of airflow. We do this by discovering exactly where the interruption happens in the articulators and by finding the most efficient way of articulating that consonant.

For example, the consonants [b] and [p] are formed only by the lips, but people often close the jaw to articulate them. Closing the jaw tends to increase breath pressure at the glottal level, thus interrupting the breath, both in the voice and at the point of formation (the lips). We can train ourselves to articulate the [b] and the [p] so that the interruption of the air happens only at the point where the lips touch, thus minimizing interruption of airflow or entangling the vocal folds.

Conductors often ask singers to "spit out" the consonants, to enunciate them as crisply as possible, which tends to tighten the jaw and interrupt airflow. If we learn to separate the function of the articulators when saying consonants, just as we do when defining vowels, we will be able to maintain a sense of legato and free-flowing air, no matter what word we are singing. I don't mean to advocate sloppy diction or dropping of consonants; on the contrary, the clarity of the consonants is actually enhanced by this airflow.

In certain languages, understandability is based on length of the consonant. Particularly in Italian, we are taught the importance of double and single consonants. Depending on how long we hold a particular consonant, the word can have a completely different meaning. Double consonants exist in English as well; for example, when one syllable or word ends with [t] and the next one begins with [t], as in the words "hat table," we normally don't pronounce both [t]'s individually in the middle of those two words; instead, we just elongate the [t] sound into a double consonant, so "hat table" becomes [hæt:e:ɪbəl], rather than [hæt te:ɪbəl]. Doubling consonants this way is essential for legato singing. Listen to Audio Sample 18 for an example of doubling consonants.

AUDIO SAMPLE 18: Double Consonants

The problem with double consonants is that we are tempted to make them too heavy while singing, particularly in Italian, which increases the pressure on the voice. This pressure on the voice interrupts at the glottal level, which minimizes airflow. We should never hold double consonants a millisecond longer than is necessary for clarity. Another common pitfall for English speakers singing in Italian is making single consonants so heavy that they sound like double consonants. This interrupts the airflow unnecessarily and makes the language inauthentic.

No matter the language, word, or syllable, we must always keep the interruption of airflow from consonants to a minimum while maintaining understandability. In some cases, we can give enough of the impression of a consonant that the word is clearly understandable, but the airflow is minimally interrupted. Some of those solutions are listed here. The final [l] and [r] listed are as we speak them in American English.

Hard [g] and [dʒ]—think of them as more nonvoiced (toward [k] or [tʃ]), which will allow the air to flow through more freely.

Final [l]—suggest the [l] by substituting an open [ʊ].

Final [r]—suggest the sound of [r] in an accented syllable by substituting the [ø] and in an unaccented syllable by substituting [œ].

Listen to Audio Sample 19 for an examples.

AUDIO SAMPLE 19: Consonant Substitutions

Shadow Vowels

In Italian, most words end with vowels. Ending a word with a consonant is awkward for native Italian speakers. Because of this, they are unaccustomed to ending syllables with their mouths closed. For that reason, many Italian singers add what is called a "shadow vowel" after a syllable that ends in a consonant. For example, the word *con* (Italian for "with") is often pronounced [konə]. Shadow vowels are undefined vowels (usually [ə]) that do not keep the airflow on a consistent path. The vowels become unaligned, destroying the legato line. Normally, we shouldn't sing any sound that is not part of the language.

The most common final consonant in Italian is [n], so the best Italian coaches will tell singers to change the final [n] into a sound that flows into the following consonant. For example, the Italian word *ingrato* becomes [iŋgrato] instead of "in-uh-grato." Another example is the phrase "in Parigi" which becomes [imparidʒi] instead of "in-uh-parigi." In the word *infelice*, the [n] should be formed with the upper teeth touching the lower lip in a sound similar to [m]. This [m]-like sound will flow directly into the following consonant, which is the same articulator position as [f]. A coach I once worked with calls this "the chipmunk [n]" because the upper teeth look like a chipmunk's teeth when one says it.

Ending a word with a consonant is not awkward for native English speakers, yet native speakers still use shadow vowels occasionally, even when singing in English. This problem may stem from diction coaches who encourage the use of the shadow vowel to hear the final consonant more clearly. The principal way to avoid this habit is to sing through all the final consonants while connecting to the following initial consonants without opening the mouth, which is what causes the shadow vowel. If the legato line is maintained, the resultant airflow will still catapult the consonant out to the audience and transmit clearly.

For example, the phrase "in the" is often sung "in-a-the" when they should be sung "inthe" without any break or shadow vowel in between the consonants. Connecting the consonants in this way keeps the words clear and maintains a legato line. When a word ends in [d], a shadow vowel is necessary to understand the consonant. Still, it is better if the singer chooses a shadow vowel that maintains a higher position of the tongue so that vowel alignment remains consistent. The word *God* would sound like "God-[ɪ]" rather than "God-uh." In some cases eliminating the final [d] makes the text more easily understood. I prefer hearing someone sing "this an' that" rather than "this and-uh that."

Even consonant clusters should seem to be part of the airflow, rather than interruptions. For example, if we are singing the words "bridge blue," the tendency is to sing, "bridge-a-ba-loo." Even though we must close our mouths to say the consonants in those words, if we imagine that the air flows through that cluster of consonants, there is a minimal interruption of the airflow, and the consonants are again catapulted to the audience.

In summary, the most important principle in defining both vowels and consonants is maintaining a legato line. When singing any piece of music, we must think hard about where and how the legato line is interrupted by the consonants and then seek to minimize that interruption in every way possible. This is the first and most important consideration in applying technique to repertoire. So when vowel definition guides our breath to flow freely through the resonators and the consonants interrupt that flow minimally, the voice will have much more color, flexibility, and communicative power.

DICTION

Most college-age voice students are required to take diction classes in which they learn to correctly pronounce Italian, German, French, and English. Diction training can be detrimental to free singing, however. The term *diction* suggests hyper-enunciation—the way we speak when talking to a small child—with very slow, overpronounced syllables, making sure that every word is clear and understandable.

Diction, in that sense, is what I call "anti-legato." Overpronouncing vowels and "spitting out" consonants cause tension and interrupt the airflow. Also, and more important, singers can have perfect diction (i.e., every consonant is crisp and every vowel is defined correctly) and listeners still have difficulty understanding what is being said. This happens when diction becomes the end goal instead of a means to an end. Singers must understand that the purpose of good diction is to make the text understandable to people who speak the language in which they are singing. Native speakers do not overenunciate their words when speaking, so if we overenunciate when singing, it actually makes the words more difficult to understand.

Sometimes if I focus very hard, I can understand every word a singer is saying, but I don't sense the meaning of what they are saying. That is because meaning and emotional intent happen at a much deeper level than diction. For example, I have seen reviews of operas by Benjamin Britten (always sung in English), in which the reviewer criticized the bad diction of the singers. I saw those same productions, and the singers' diction was fabulous—every word was understandable. The problem with Britten's texts is that they are so metaphorical and poetic that even the most perfectly pronounced diction will not, on its own, convey the meaning of the words. In his operas the music helps convey the meaning, beyond (and sometimes in contradiction to) what is being said by the characters. The music tells much of the story, so if we only catch a word here and there when listening, we will likely understand the emotional intent of the piece. However, it is best when the meaning is clear in the singers' minds and their diction makes the words understandable, too.

In opera, the syntax and flow of language is often different from regular conversation. The listener, therefore, may have difficulty understanding what is being said even if the singer's production makes it sound like conversational speech. Librettists deal with this challenge all the time—how to convey the deeper meaning in a scene or situation while using as few words as possible.

Often that entails using words that are not a part of everyday speech, which makes immediate understandability difficult. That has nothing to do with diction. The key for singers is to look beneath the pronunciation of the words to assess the emotional truth of the situation—the composer's intent—and then use legato technique, diction, facial expression, acting, and musical expressiveness to convey that idea with as much clarity as possible.

MUSICALITY

I saw a production of *The Marriage of Figaro* in which many of the women in the cast sang flat much of the time. In a discussion about this issue with some of my colleagues, the question was raised about whether the women's poor intonation was a hearing issue—if they were hearing the pitch flat in their heads. I believe poor intonation is seldom a hearing problem because singers are the only musicians who must hear a pitch in their heads before they can even approximate it. If a trumpeter wants to play an A, he can press down the first two valves and use a certain tightness of the lips and he will produce something close to an A. Likewise, a violinist knows where to press down on the strings for a specific pitch, but she doesn't actually have to hear the pitch before she plays it.

Of course, good instrumentalists develop the ability to hear a pitch before they play it, but a singer has no other option. We cannot even approximate the pitch without hearing it first. When singers are unable to tell that they are out of tune, they are proving that intonation problems are a result of improper vocal production. If the voice is balanced and free, the pitch will be perfect, or at least as perfect as it is in the singer's head before beginning to sing.

Singing on pitch is considered a basic tenet of musicianship, but there is a difference between musicianship and musicality. Musicianship is accurately demonstrating what is on the page—correct rhythms, pitches, tempos, and dynamic markings. Musicality, on the other hand, is giving expressiveness to the elements of musicianship.

The qualities most people associate with being "musical" include phrasing, shaping the phrase, performing varying dynamics, showing variety of colors in the sound, and demonstrating appropriate give and take of tempo. These elements, which seem to give emotion and expressiveness to the music, are inherent to the vocal instrument.

For example, in an effort to be musical, a pianist is expected to begin the five-tone scale C-D-E-F-G-F-E-D-C softly, then crescendo as the scale ascends and decrescendo on the way back down. A singer, on the other hand, requires no manipulated dynamic shift of that sort. When a singer sings the same scale, the vocal folds must become longer and tighter for higher pitches and shorter and looser for lower pitches, which creates a natural dynamic shift. Therefore the phrase sounds inherently musical without any intention of changing the dynamics.

When violinists phrase, they "breathe" by gently lifting the bow off of the strings and then reengaging the string with renewed energy. Their phrasing is an imitation of the natural way a singer breathes, and it is considered a hallmark of musicality. A violinist will vary the speed of the vibrato according to the mood of the music. For relaxing, languid music, they slow the movement of their hand to affect the vibrato speed, and in contrast speed up the vibrato for exciting, intense music. These changes of vibrato speed are inherent to singers, who, without intending to, change the speed of vibrato according to the emotional intent of the music they are singing.

Because singers make sounds through words, the variety of vowels and emotions associated with the word meanings naturally cause a variety of color in the timbre. Again, instrumentalists are trying to imitate what is natural to the singer in giving color variety. With singers variations in tempo also happen naturally in conjunction with the mood of the piece and the breath demands of the phrase. These hallmarks of musicality are things that singers simply *must* do so that the voice can function properly. This is why I tell my students that the most musical thing they can do is to sing well—musicality happens on its own because the human voice naturally oozes it.

Singers often come from a background of instrumental training, so they attempt to be musical in the same way a violinist or pianist does. This superimposes the instrumentalist's kind of musicality onto a naturally musical instrument. I tell singers that they are imitating an instrumentalist imitating a singer. All they really need to do is sing freely with intention, and the voice will naturally have all kinds of musicality. Sometimes singers' attempts to be musical make their voices tense and tight, so I half-jokingly tell them to stop being musical and just sing!

> Coming from an instrumental background (viola), I carry a lot of baggage. Sometimes I sing as if the words don't exist and I phrase as if I were playing instead of singing. I have had to find a more raw, larger and more flowing sound. I've learned to sing like a singer.
>
> Christopher Herbert, baritone

DYNAMICS: HOW TO SING SOFTLY

When asked how to sing softly, Inez Silberg once told a student, "Imagine you are walking across a field of snow without making any footprints." When her student told me about that analogy, I thought it made a lot of sense even though the singer felt it was one of the stupidest things she had ever heard. Of course that analogy contains no specific, practical, physiological explanation of what we do to sing softly, but as a metaphor for the physiological process of singing softly, it makes perfect sense. In nonmetaphorical terms, to sing softly, we just maintain consistent airflow while decreasing the intensity of the phonation.

So how do we know when to sing softly? When making choices about dynamics, singers should first consider why the composer gave a specific dynamic indication in the music. Certainly the composer did not intend a specific decibel level, so the question is, what was the emotional or dramatic intent of that dynamic marking? Often, a dynamic shift suggests more of a change in color or intensity and not necessarily a variance in decibel levels.

That said, singers must learn to sing softly. Most singers heading for opera careers have big voices, so they have a history of having choir directors shushing them, telling them to hold back their voices. We learn, literally, to *hold back* our air and develop a habit of decreasing airflow and increasing tension whenever we sing softly. Unfortunately, decreased airflow and increased tension are the opposite of what we need to do to sing softly.

Mrs. Silberg once told me that to sing a decrescendo, "You should imagine that the person you are talking to is walking toward you, so you don't have to project as much to get him to hear you." On a technical level, that means that when we sing softly, we let the air flow just as freely as when singing loudly, but we simply don't use as much voice. We start with a fully engaged voice, keep the air flowing freely and gradually decrease the weight, presence, or intensity of the voice. The key is to always maintain a steady stream of air flowing through the voice, whatever the level of intensity of phonation.

To crescendo (or get louder), then, we speed up the airflow without increasing vocal resistance. This elevated air intensity causes the vocal folds to respond with wider undulation. By intensifying the flow of air through the voice, we get more response from the voice without forcing the air through. We just release the air as usual and allow the airflow to speed up for louder passages. Listen to Audio Sample 20 for an example.

 AUDIO SAMPLE 20: Crescendo and Decrescendo

AGILITY AND *FIORATURA*

In The Wobble we gain the basic skill of agility. We learn to keep the vocal cords loose and feeling flabby, maintaining a steady flow of air so that we sing every pitch clearly and freely. The rubber meets the road with this skill when we have to apply it to learning *fioratura* passages. *Fioratura* is defined as "the flowery, embellished vocal line within a piece of music." *Fioratura* occurs most frequently in music by Mozart, Bach, Handel, and the *bel canto* Italian composers, of whom Rossini, Donizetti, and Bellini are the most famous. *Fioratura* passages may include rapid scales, arpeggios, varying intervals, or repeated musical motives normally on the same vowel. In The Wobble, we alternate on intervals of a fourth, but in *fioratura* passages, we have to negotiate intervals of every stripe.

People often say that bigger, heavier voices are not expected to sing *fioratura* passages well, but lighter voices are. Obviously, lighter, smaller voices can normally move more quickly and easily through these passages because they have a lot less mass to maneuver; however, the technique of keeping the vocal cords flexible, no matter their length or thickness, is crucial to vocal health and longevity. The difference is that lighter voices can be tense and still have a certain amount of agility, whereas bigger, thicker voices cannot be tense and have any agility at all. If lighter voices sang *fioratura* without tension, their voices would be even more agile and would make richer sound. Tension, or entanglement of the voice, is what makes singing these passages difficult, so any voice that can sing without tension or entanglement will be able to sing *fioratura* passages well.

The most common mistake in singing *fioratura* is trying to physically articulate every note. That usually entails pulsing the abdomen while squeezing the adductor muscles on each pulse. This can give the impression of control, but it actually causes tension. Good coloratura singing (pertaining to great feats of agility, fast singing, high singing, trills, embellishments, and the like) should feel like smooth legato singing.

The most common approach to singing *fioratura* passages is to "lighten up the voice" or take the weight out of the voice. I don't believe we should ever sing with weight in the voice in the first place, so this idea doesn't work for me. I have developed a five-step process for learning *fioratura* passages, without changing the overall legato approach to singing.

Step One: Divide into Pulses

The first step in learning a *fioratura* passage is to divide it into pulses. The pulses in the passage often coincide with the beats. For example, let's look at this *fioratura* passage from Handel's *Messiah*:

Rage - - - - - - - - - - - - - - - - -

Music Example 10.1. *Fioratura* Passage

We divide this passage into pulses and sing the note at the beginning of each pulse on a detached vowel, like so:

MUSIC EXAMPLE 10.2. *Fioratura* Step 1

We sing the pulses on a *detached* vowel because, as we learned in Spontaneous Combustion, it forces us to immediately phonate with freedom and clarity. That way, we get the sensation of how the voice should feel on each of those pulses when it is balanced and free. Listen to Audio Sample 21 to hear this demonstrated.

AUDIO SAMPLE 21: Divide into Pulses

Step Two: Sing the Pulses with Legato

Starting with a pulse that is slower than performance tempo, we connect all of these pitches, like so:

MUSIC EXAMPLE 10.3. *Fioratura* Step 2

AUDIO SAMPLE 22: Sing the Pulses with Legato

Step Three: Sing All the Notes, Pulse by Pulse

Next, we sing all of the notes in one pulse and the first note of the next pulse at a slower tempo, like so:

MUSIC EXAMPLE 10.4. *Fioratura* Step 3

 AUDIO SAMPLE 23: Sing All the Notes Pulse by Pulse

Step Four: Combine Two Pulses at a Time

Now, we combine two pulses plus the first note of the next pulse at a slower tempo, like so:

MUSIC EXAMPLE 10.5. *Fioratura* Step 4

 AUDIO SAMPLE 24: Combine Two Pulses at a Time

Step Five: Combine All Pulses

In the final step, we sing all of the notes of every pulse. Once we can do so with freedom and clarity, we gradually increase the speed to performance tempo. Listen to Audio Sample 25 to hear this demonstrated.

MUSIC EXAMPLE 10.6. *Fioratura* Step 5

 AUDIO SAMPLE 25: Combine All Pulses

This five-step process is also demonstrated with the following passage from Rossini's *Il Barbiere di Siviglia*. Listen to Audio Sample 26 to hear this demonstrated.

MUSIC EXAMPLE 10.7. Rossini *Fioratura* Passage

 AUDIO SAMPLE 26: Five-Step Process on Rossini

By going through this process with every *fioratura* passage, we will learn the passage so that it always feels like we are only singing the pulses in the phrase. But because we have learned all the notes, they will sound clear and free.

After singers have mastered the ability to sing *fioratura* with legato, I sometimes teach them to articulate the notes with "supraglottal" aspiration (like the sound Woody Woodpecker makes). Calling it supraglottal is a misnomer because obviously it happens in the glottis itself, but it feels supraglottal because it has no subglottal pressure. Doing supraglottal aspiration makes each note even clearer, but it should not be attempted until the singer has fully mastered the legato technique in singing *fioratura* passages. Listen to Audio Sample 27 for an example.

 AUDIO SAMPLE 27: Supraglottal Aspiration in *Fioratura*

SINGING STACCATO (WITH LEGATO)

Staccato is an Italian word that means "detached." Many people think *staccato* means "short," so they start a note and immediately cut it off. Even when we sing detached or staccato notes, we should maintain a legato technique, or a consistent flow of air. We do this by making the detachment a supraglottal (not a subglottal) sensation. We begin singing a continuous [ɑ] and repeat the [ɑ] with minimal glottal interruption, as demonstrated in Audio Sample 28.

AUDIO SAMPLE 28: Staccato/Legato [ɑ]'s

Each note ends as the next one begins—with a glottal onset. When we separate the notes this way, it feels like the air is not really stopping at all but flowing steadily through the entire phrase. Normal attempts to sing staccato often entail squeezing the glottis closed to stop each note, then keeping it closed tight, which stops the airflow.

A perfect example of how to apply this technique to repertoire is a passage from the Queen of the Night's aria from Mozart's *The Magic Flute*. I have my students sing this passage as one continuous phrase with a new onset on each note instead of the more common approach of doing a glottal stop and start between the notes. Accomplishing this is not easy, but doing so makes for easier and healthier singing, not to mention longer careers! Listen to Audio Sample 29 for an example.

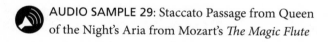

AUDIO SAMPLE 29: Staccato Passage from Queen of the Night's Aria from Mozart's *The Magic Flute*

DEALING WITH WIDE INTERVALS

Wide intervals present another challenge to legato technique. Every time we change intervals we are more likely to stop, readjust, and interrupt the legato line. The wider the interval, the more likely we are to be afraid of it, hold the voice, and stop the airflow. The key is to find a way to maintain a consistent airflow while singing pitches far apart. The Wobble Invention is designed to keep the cords loose and the breath steady when singing wide intervals. An additional way through this challenge is to make the note before the higher note feel breathier in the throat. By doing so, we maintain a consistent breath flow, and we don't have to push out any more air to "support" the higher note. Making the voice breathier before a wide interval is a conditioning technique. Eventually the process will become second nature, and we will automatically channel the air into a breathier sensation on the note before the high pitch of a wide ascending interval.

When we are singing a phrase that drops to a lower pitch, we face a similar challenge—the common tendency is to diminish the airflow when we shift to lower pitches. In that scenario, we don't make the voice breathier before going down; instead, we maintain airflow on the lower note as we descend. We must also not flatten the vowel as we shift down, but keep the vowel in a high sigh-like place, even as we sing lower pitches. The most important principle in negotiating intervals is to make the entire phrase feel like there is no change as we sing through the phrase—that we are in automatic transmission, not manual transmission, so the intervals feel seamless and balanced.

Dealing with Stylistic Differences in Music

There is a general assumption that Mozart is good for all singers because his music requires a clear and pure tone quality. Because of the transparent nature of Mozart's music, singers typically don't sing it heavily. Audition panels also like to hear Mozart because it demands simplicity and refinement. Although it is true that the style of Mozart's music requires a clear, pure quality, there is an assumption that other styles of music and other composers do not require that quality. There is also an assumption that we should sing Mozart differently than we sing other styles or periods of music. I disagree with these assumptions.

Free vocalism is good vocalism; we should sing freely, with our own voice, whatever the style of music we happen to be singing. Learning to demonstrate stylistic differences is a matter of study—working with coaches, studying music literature and style, and listening to recordings while paying close attention to changes in style across the different musical periods. By studying and listening, we absorb stylistic changes and can apply them when singing different styles of music. But that doesn't mean we should change our vocalism for those different styles.

Because of the stylistic demands of Mozart's music, smaller voices more easily sound pure and clear when singing it with their own voice. Therefore people have come to expect smaller voices singing Mozart. But any size voice that can sing purely and clearly—to which all voice sizes should aspire —can be successful in Mozart's music. The problem comes when people who have large voices try to hold back or pinch their voices to sound stylistically appropriate for Mozart. Conversely, because the style of verismo music (Puccini, Mascagni, Leoncavallo, Giordano) requires a warm, lush, fuller sound, smaller voices are tempted to push beyond what is healthy for them. The style of music appropriate for different voice types has as much to do with the thickness of the orchestral texture as anything else. That is why singing Mozart's music can be potentially as harmful as singing Puccini, depending on the vocal approach. A dramatic voice that holds back to sing Mozart can do as much vocal damage as a lyric voice that pushes to sing Puccini.

Of course, a lush, big, resonant sound is ideal for Puccini. The problem is that many singers try to make their voices sound like "Puccini voices" or "Mozart voices" or "Verdi voices" instead of just singing with their true voices in any repertoire. I don't believe there is such a thing as a 'Mozart voice' or a 'Puccini voice' or a 'Verdi voice.' The audience, critics, or producers make those kinds of categorizations, but I think singers should always sing with their true voice. Singers who believe in those categorizations can limit their possibilities and restrict their vocal production, thinking their voices are appropriate to only one style or composer. Singers should sing freely with their own voices; when they do, the correct repertoire will reveal itself in time. We will discuss this more in the next chapter.

SINGING NONCLASSICAL STYLES

My theory is that the biggest difference between classical, Broadway, country, R&B, and popular music—or any style of music for that matter—has more to do with the use of the language than the use of the voice. The way language is used in musical theater, country music, and classical music differs greatly from genre to genre. Musical theater singers typically use a middle American accent much like TV or radio broadcasters (unless they are trying to create a character with a specific regional dialect). Country music uses a Southern dialect. Popular music generally uses a middle American accent, with different stylistic elements like holding the tone for a few beats before letting the vibrato come in and sliding up to initial pitches. Classical music uses more of a high British-English usage, which generally has darker, higher vowels, more legato, and clearer articulation of consonants.

If the major difference among nonclassical styles is use of the language, we can assume that the basic vocalism should not be altered. In other words, it is possible to sing any style freely. Other styles won't be as free as a fully balanced classical sound where vowels are formed with a refinement that enhances airflow and contributes to a more resonant quality. In nonclassical styles, we flatten the vowels to varying degrees, which can cause downward pressure on the voice. But we can learn to sing with the same honesty and integrity, even without the same resonance that classical music demands.

Some of the younger generation may not be aware that electric amplification of singers is a modern phenomenon and that opera/classical singers still are not normally amplified. Because nowadays all other singers (pop, musical theater, country, etc.) are almost always amplified, many young people express astonishment and disbelief when told that opera singers perform without such assistance. Amplification helps explain why pop and musical theater singers can get away with flatter vowels and less resonance. Refined vowels, enhanced airflow, and greater resonance are essential to projecting a voice in a large concert hall or opera house.

If we learn to sing with the alignment and freedom necessary for classical music, our ability to sing freely in other styles is greatly enhanced. In that sense, classical singing is the top of the hierarchy of musical styles. Those who have learned to sing freely for classical style should be able to adapt their technique to sing country, Broadway, or popular music. However, high-level country, Broadway, and popular singers seldom have the technique to sing classical music. The more freedom we attain in our phonation (through correct definition of vowels and airflow), the freer we will be to sing in any style we want.

The Broadway "Belt"

In the musical theater world, singers have developed a technique commonly known as *belting*. What most people consider a successful belt is using chest voice as high as possible. Women, more than men, are taught to keep the voice in chest register as they ascend, flattening the vowels, pinching the cords, and pressing their air against their cords as they go up into the higher range. Smaller, lighter voices usually belt best because their smaller cords allow them to carry this chest adjustment higher than most. Deeper, lower, and bigger voices have much more difficulty belting very high because they simply can't carry that kind of weight into the upper range.

A healthy approach to belting is to try to keep air flowing through the voice, despite using flatter, brighter vowels. I try to get singers not to think in terms of chest versus head voice because qualities of both (phonation and airflow) should be present to some degree in all ranges of the voice. When I teach musical theater singers, I try to get them to have some degree of phonation and airflow present throughout their range.

I allow musical theater singers to carry the chest voice higher than normal by using a brighter vowel but still with free-flowing air. The resulting sound can pass as a belt because it has "cut," but it is not pure chest voice. Again, it is worth the effort required to learn to sing with a classical legato technique, even for belters, because the freedom gained in that process can be modified to sing a healthy belt or any other style of music.

One of my students brought a musical theater piece to work on in a lesson. He had sung some musical theater pieces for me early in our work together when his voice and body were very tense. To help him free his voice, I made him sing only classical music for a period of time, after which I was amazed at the new-found freedom in his voice when he started singing the musical theater pieces again. By simply changing the quality of his vowels, he could sing in a Broadway style while maintaining the freedom he had gained from learning a legato technique.

One of my pet peeves is when opera singers sing Broadway or popular music and still sound like opera singers. Without adapting the use of the language and the height of the vowels, the sound is pretentious and annoying. This approach causes musical theater professionals to think that all opera singers are just making pretty sounds and not communicating. Singing in any style should have the same goal—telling the story. All singers should be communicating something, no matter what they are singing. In classical music and opera, the music normally communicates the drama, so the sound of the singer's voice becomes part of the music and therefore the drama. Because of this, it is not as crucial for the opera singer to convey the message as it is for singers of other styles.

In musical theater, it is essential for the singer/actor to tell the story because the music is designed more to accompany and enhance the drama than to convey the message. It is therefore incumbent upon these performers to imbue their singing with the drama and communicate with much more than just their voices. However, any performer who communicates honestly through acting and singing will give a compelling performance regardless of the genre. A person can produce free, healthy, beautiful singing sounds and still be a great actor—communicating with integrity and authenticity. That is why opera and musical theater are essentially the same art. The singer/actor should not change singing technique from one style to the other. He or she should only change the way he or she uses the language.

11

Find Your Own Path

Once singers have established a solid technique and are committed to the process of continual improvement, many decide to pursue a professional career in singing. I am often asked how one goes about achieving a successful career as a singer. There is no easy answer to that question because all of the singers I have worked with who have achieved what many would call a successful career have attained their success by following very different paths. The most important principle in pursuing any career should be the same as the principle involved in learning to sing: Be true to yourself.

In the Inventions, we uncover our naked voice and learn to use that voice with freedom, flexibility, and power. Through that process we discover our uniqueness—that quality of sound or communicative gift that is ours alone. We learn how to be ourselves fully and openly, and we must continue on that path as we pursue a career. Unless we remain true to ourselves, we are destined for disappointment or confusion.

I have worked with singers at every stage of professional development—from beginning student to world-famous opera star—for more than thirty years. During that time I have observed that those who stay true to themselves have longer, more fulfilling careers than those who don't. Many people in the classical music business are happy to offer career advice, telling singers to whom they need to be connected, how they need to dress, where they should train, how to create a good résumé, how to get a good headshot, and so on. The most common and pervasive form of this advice comes when coaches, directors, conductors, and teachers tell singers what repertoire they should sing.

CHOOSING APPROPRIATE REPERTOIRE

Because of what is known as the *fach* system (*fach* is a German word that means "box or division") in which specific voice types are assigned a specific set of roles and repertoire, singers are led to believe that the choice of repertoire will make or break them. I firmly disagree with this point of view. When we get our voices working well and we are singing with our true sound, the right repertoire will emerge naturally. This concept flies in the face of what many in the business seem to believe. When choosing repertoire, the work we have done in discovering who we are becomes crucially important. We must know who we are and what we are about in order to maintain our integrity in the face of often overwhelming and contradictory advice from those in power in the professional world.

The most important consideration is not what repertoire we sing but how we sing it. There is nothing inherent about any piece of music that ensures our comfort or success in auditions. All the focus on voice types and *fachs* has more to do with marketing than with what is healthy or right for each singer. All singers should seek to find music they connect to and that speaks to them personally. If it is not a good choice, they will know it, and in honoring their own intuition they will probably choose not to sing it. But that process must be an individual one; it cannot be dictated by anyone other than the singers themselves.

The music business wants us to present ourselves as a package that is easy to market. They want to sell a "dramatic soprano," a "Verdi baritone," or a "Mozart tenor." When we are singers of a certain age and a basic quality of sound with a physical look to match, we are put into a box that defines us for the rest of our careers. We are pegged, pigeonholed, and stuffed into a specific category that might have nothing to do with who we are as people or singers. I call this the "*fach* box" (beware of mispronunciation!) and we must break out of it. We must dare to be unique and find the repertoire that is uniquely right for us.

I taught a thirty-year-old student who was working on a graduate diploma and was ready to begin his professional career. He was constantly asking me what he should sing in auditions, and I told him—as I tell everyone—that the most important thing to decide is what music you truly love and want to sing. Finding the answer to that question is far more important than presenting yourself in a particular category. Most people would have pegged him as a "character bass." It wasn't a huge, lush bass sound, but he did have great low notes, along with a personality that was a bit quirky. All of those qualities work very nicely for character bass roles. I told him he shouldn't just go through the repertoire books and choose character bass arias and expect to make a good presentation. He should choose pieces that he really connects to, whether or not they fit the character bass *fach*.

He was shocked at this advice. No one had ever told him what I think is the most obvious idea in the world—choose repertoire that you love and that you want to sing. So he did what I suggested, chose five arias that he loved, that he connected to, and that fit his voice well, and he won the district Met auditions that year with those arias. He told me he was convinced he won because he loved and was excited to sing every piece on his list.

It is true that singers should be sensitive to marketing issues and think about how to market themselves to get work as singers. But the most important thing is to find repertoire that we love. As we grow and change, our repertoire will also grow and change. Some arias we sing in our early twenties may remain relevant to us throughout our lives, and some may become favorites over time. Sometimes we will be drawn to an aria, try to sing it, and find it terribly difficult, or we don't identify with it. Ten years later, that aria might feel totally free and easy, and our life experiences then enable us to connect with it on a much deeper level. We must remain flexible and true to ourselves throughout our lives and careers, and not just assume that an aria that was right for us at twenty will be right for us at forty and vice versa.

The industry standard for auditions and competitions is for every singer to have five or six arias of various styles, musical periods, and languages (usually one each in Italian, French, German, English, and at least one aria by Mozart, with contrasting pieces from the Baroque, Classical, Romantic, and contemporary periods). This is all part of marketing, and to some degree we should try to meet those expectations. However, I know singers who list three Italian arias, one German, and one English, and the companies for which they audition have had no complaints. We don't have to be a master of every style of music, although we should study and try all kinds to discover what music we connect to most. We will not love every kind of music equally, so we must constantly find pieces in whatever style or period that speaks to us and that we connect to—we must fly in the face of the marketing expectations of the business. If the only music we connect to is Italian *bel canto* opera, then we should list five *bel canto* arias, with as much variety among them as possible (unless, of course, the requirements for the audition ask for something different).

Many people would disagree with me on this point because they think singers will choose repertoire that is too heavy or unhealthy for them to sing. However, as we gain freedom and flexibility in our technique, we won't want to sing pieces that are difficult or unhealthy because they won't be fun to sing. We might connect to that music, but if we can't pull it off in performance because it is vocally uncomfortable, we won't want to sing it. Instead, we will want to sing things that feel good in our voice and that are comfortable to perform. By being true to ourselves, we will automatically eliminate an unhealthy aria from our repertoire. Sometimes we will discover music that speaks to us deeply but that we don't feel comfortable singing.

In my own singing career, I found that my natural sound and vocal timbre had the ring and brightness of a tenor and the weight, richness, and depth of a baritone, yet without any bass quality. Now, when I sing art songs or pieces that don't require a lot of dramatic intensity, people often suspect I'm a tenor (even though I sing in the baritone key and can't sustain a tenor tessitura). But when I sing operatic repertoire, the increased energy adds a richer, deeper quality to my sound, and people easily accept that I am a baritone. It's not that I am changing the way I sing; rather, the amount of energy I infuse into the music makes the difference. Recitals are more intimate and usually in smaller venues, so I naturally don't engage my voice with as much intensity as I would in a large hall over an orchestra.

My personal experience has led me to believe, therefore, that voice category labels are at best subjective and often meaningless. People will adhere to varying opinions regarding our voice category and what kind of repertoire we should be singing. The only constant, the one thing we should hold onto, is staying true to ourselves—singing with our own true, free voice. When we sing music that speaks to us, we reconnect with our original source of utterance.

Music professionals, particularly non-voice teachers, are constantly telling singers what repertoire they should or should not sing. People who audition for opera companies, competitions, or agents often get feedback about what repertoire they should sing, as if somehow by choosing the right repertoire people will become good or successful singers. Most of those professionals mean well. They hear a certain sound and they think that particular sound would fit a particular role well, based on other voices they have heard live or on recordings. Sometimes their advice can be very valuable in helping singers find music that they connect to and should sing. Many vocal coaches are immense resources of knowledge about repertoire, so I advise my students to seek those coaches' advice about what might work well for their voice. Often they can suggest things that singers might never have discovered on their own, and in that case their advice is important and sometimes essential.

However, the important thing for singers to remember, even when consulting with the best coaches in the world, is that the choice of repertoire is not what makes or breaks you as a singer—*how* you sing will ultimately make the difference. For example, the aria "Dich teure Halle" from Wagner's opera *Tannhäuser* has a range from D4 up to B5 and is normally sung by a dramatic soprano. But female singers of all voice types can negotiate that range. And if any of those voice types really love it and want to sing it, I would say, "Go for it!" I don't mean that this aria would be appropriate for all voice types to perform, but singing it for the pleasure of private audiences and ourselves is not necessarily going to be damaging. However, if a singer is not a dramatic soprano and tries to sound like one, she will hurt herself. Whatever we sing, we have to sing with our own voice and our own technique and not try to sound like someone or something we are not.

The challenge in choosing repertoire is the singer's perception of any given piece. If we want to sing a dramatic aria, and we have preconceived notions of what that "dramatic" quality should be but it is not our natural quality, we must be very careful that we use our own voice and personality. If we do that, we may actually change the listener's concept of what the aria should sound like. Most professionals do have an idea of what a particular aria should sound like. They have heard these operas many times, and they have a certain sound in their mind of the weight, size, and color of voice for every role. Sometimes it is a standardized opinion, but often it is unique to that person. Either way, those who listen to auditions come to the process with a specific notion of what a voice should sound like in any given aria, and they will only cast singers who fit that notion. However, I have known singers who audition with arias that don't necessarily fit that notion, but because they engage the piece so uniquely and infuse it with so much of their own insight and personality, they change people's ideas of what those roles should sound like.

It is also important to remember that the singing business itself goes through phases, and ideas change from time to time regarding what kind of voice should sing particular roles. For example, a generation ago, the title role of Bizet's *Carmen* was often sung by sopranos and lyric mezzos because Carmen's range is not extremely high or low. Almost any female can sing Carmen's actual notes. Recently, the reigning Carmen in the world has been Denyce Graves. I have seen her perform this opera, and I like her interpretation as well as any I have ever seen. But only Denyce Graves can sing Carmen like Denyce Graves. Others who try to sing the role and sound like her are going to hurt themselves and sound terrible because there is only one Denyce Graves. I truly believe that a variety of sopranos and mezzos of all types could sing Carmen well if they sing it with their own voice and connect to the character, although it does require strength and projection in the middle register.

Another example of changing notions about the casting of roles is the women in Mozart's *Don Giovanni*. When I first heard the opera performed, the role of Donna Elvira was cast as a spinto, or heavier-voiced soprano, and that of Donna Anna was a lighter, lyric soprano. Now it seems Donna Anna is usually a spinto soprano and Elvira is a full lyric (but not dramatic) soprano or occasionally a lyric mezzo. Sometimes a great singer will come along and because she sings with such beauty, power, freedom, and integrity, she changes people's concept of what kind of voice should sing a particular role. As a result, her interpretation affects an entire generation of singers.

Composer Carlisle Floyd has been quoted saying that his preference for most of his leading ladies is "a voice like Tebaldi in a body like Scarlet O'Hara's." Because those two qualities rarely happen in the same person, the title character in his opera *Susannah* has been cast with every voice type from coloratura to dramatic soprano. One of my students, a gorgeous coloratura soprano, was cast in the role of Susannah while studying at Florida State in a production Floyd was directing. In working with her on the role, he suggested some alternate, higher pitches in the aria "The Trees on the Mountain," based on her unique vocal qualities. She later used those alternate pitches when singing that aria in a competition and was criticized by the judges. These particular judges had also previously done the opera with Floyd, and they told this soprano that he would insist that she "only sing the pitches written on the page!" This is an example of how people in the business get set in their minds how things are supposed to be, and they start to pigeonhole singers unnecessarily. We must challenge that tendency and stay true to ourselves.

Adjudicators of competitions, myself included, often make assumptions about singers based on the repertoire on their list. When we see a singer's list, we think we already know what his or her voice will sound like. We box people in. Most singers are aware of that, so they choose arias based on what kind of voice they think the judges will want to hear—they box themselves in. If we sing the arias well and engage with them in a meaningful way, we might be cast in a variety of unexpected roles.

Consider the following scenario: A woman comes into an audition and lists the following arias—The Habañera from *Carmen*, "Vissi d'arte" from *Tosca*, and "Je suis Titania" from *Mignon*. The judges will likely think she has a multiple personality disorder and has no idea who she really is. Carmen is a sultry, dramatic mezzo role, Tosca is a fiery, dramatic soprano, and the *Mignon* aria is sung by a coquettish high coloratura. All three roles represent completely different *fachs*, and no one would imagine the same person singing all three appropriately. The fact is, however, that Maria Callas was world famous for all three of those roles. That is not to say that she was technically flawless or had the perfect sound for all three roles. However, she performed all three superbly, because she dared to engage herself fully in each role, singing with her own voice no matter the role or the expectations associated with that role.

We have all become so category-minded these days that it seems building a career is all about choosing the right repertoire. The problem is that every coach, conductor, and teacher will have a different opinion of what each singer's voice is and what music is appropriate to that voice. It is a never-ending, losing battle. While acknowledging the expectations of the business, we should not feel compelled to cater to those expectations but rather be true to ourselves. If singing Carmen and "Je suis Titania" both feel right and true for a soprano, then I dare her to sing both. The same company might not hire her for both roles, but one could hire her to sing Carmen and another to sing Philene (the coloratura role in *Mignon*). It all depends on their personal tastes, who else is already cast, or the kind of sounds that the casting director happens to like. It is pointless for a singer to second-guess the expectations of the people listening to auditions because everyone's opinion is different.

The task of choosing repertoire really matters only after we have done the work of uncovering the naked voice—learning to sing with free phonation and airflow. The more aligned the voice becomes, the more naturally the right repertoire will emerge. Sometimes young singers will ask me if they can sing a particular aria, and I tell them to wait a few years. If they work on that aria before their technical issues are more ironed out, they are likely to develop habits they will have to unlearn later. It is not that their instincts are wrong or that they should never sing that piece; rather, they should just wait until they are more technically secure so they won't have as much baggage to deal with when they truly are ready to sing it.

I once taught a young soprano who had a difficult time singing in her middle register. In that range, her voice was breathy and pushed, without clarity or core. The higher she sang, the more impressive and clear her voice became, so of course, she wanted to sing mostly in the higher range. She was told by a well-meaning coach that her middle-register problem came from choosing repertoire that made her blast out the top of her voice, so he advised her to sing repertoire that stayed in the middle range. I disagreed with this advice because singers can't get excited about singing pieces that feel uncomfortable and sound bad. Choosing repertoire while developing technique is tricky because we have to work on things that expose our weaknesses to fix them, but we need to perform things that we feel we can present successfully. Performing pieces that reveal weaknesses is a great way to invite discouragement. In any case, this soprano's instincts about what she should sing were much better than mine or the coach's. Forcing her to sing things only in the middle register would have killed her soul and made her not want to sing anymore.

As we develop better technique, we will come to know what repertoire is right for us. We will want to sing what is comfortable and therefore what we can do well. We won't continue to sing things that clearly are beyond our reach only to show off. Younger singers often choose arias to show how high they can sing and to impress people with the notes they can "hit." As they develop, either those notes become easier or they realize it's not fun to sing where it's uncomfortable. This motivates singers to choose repertoire more attuned to their individual voices.

In my own performing, I found that the roles and arias that motivated me to sing were the more dramatic, *verismo*, and Verdi baritone roles. But the color of my voice had more of a tenor quality and was more suited to the *bel canto* Italian repertoire. I was fully aware of this fact, but I was not motivated by the *bel canto* repertoire because I didn't connect to the music or the drama of those pieces. I sang the dramatic repertoire better because it spoke to me. The competitions I won and the attention I received as a singer always came when I sang the dramatic baritone repertoire. As I became fully aware of this disconnect between the music that spoke to me and the marketing expectations of the business (i.e., that my timbre was more suited to *bel canto*), I chose not to continue the pursuit of a professional singing career.

I remember one case in which I was a district Met competition winner, having won by singing the Prologue to *Pagliacci*. In a master class the next day with a famous operatic tenor, I offered the Prologue aria again. He asked me if I had any *bel canto* repertoire, so I offered "Bella siccome un angelo" from Donizetti's *Don Pasquale*. After I sang the first couple of phrases he stopped me and said, "This is perfect for you! This is what you should be singing." I just nodded and agreed with him, but in my head I was thinking, "Yes, but if I had sung this aria for you yesterday, I would not have won this competition." I knew that I had won because I sang something I connected to and that touched people.

We must always stay true to ourselves when choosing repertoire. Realizing that I probably couldn't sing the music that motivated me in the larger opera houses, I lost my desire to pursue a career as a singer. I chose to direct my career aspirations toward challenging singers to be true to themselves, rather than sell out to the marketing expectations of the profession.

One of my students from the southern part of this country grew up in a gospel-choir church community. He was seemingly rather successful in auditions, so his colleagues often asked him how he prepared. He said, "You gotta get that grill warmed up!" He meant that we have to be poised and focused, to have the whole body and mind in line with what we are about to do, ready to perform and express something with our voice. We have to think through our pieces and arias, and that positive mental visualization is almost as important (if not more so) than warming up the voice.

There is immense power in positive visualization. The default human tendency when we are anticipating an important event in the future is to envision every possible negative thing that could go wrong. When an audition or performance is coming up, we see ourselves tripping on stage, stumbling and falling flat on our faces, forgetting the words, or realizing halfway through the audition that our fly is unzipped. Then, because we have such a negative vision of what will happen, we have to do a lot of compensatory work to keep these things from happening.

All that negative energy sets us up for failure. I suggest that we do positive visualization before any audition or performance. We envision ourselves looking great, feeling confident, walking onstage with energy, imagining how our voice will feel at its best, and thinking about what we want to express and communicate. It is good to do this several times in meditation before the audition so that by the time the audition arrives, we already have positive memories and energy stored up—and we are bound to sing better.

Of course, positive visualization becomes easier for those who have had positive singing experiences. Many young singers go into the audition circuit before they are ready, and their energy is focused on trying to prove that they are ready. They are trying to be something they are not—yet. That attitude transmits a lot of negative energy, and that negative energy is passed on to the audition panel.

After we have worked hard to align and free our voices and we feel comfortable with our repertoire and presentation, we will naturally veer toward positive visualization. The better we sing and the more comfortable we are with our voice and who we are, the more positive experiences we will have in performing. And positive experiences generate *more* positive experiences. The ability to transform negative thoughts into positive thoughts and visualizations is rooted in our mindset and our ability to let go of expectations, accepting ourselves and just being who we are at all times.

Often singers fantasize about wowing the listener every time we open our mouths to sing, and then we are disappointed because we don't get the response we hoped for or expected. Wowing the audience will not normally be the experience every time we sing, especially at an audition. We have to change our expectations so that we are not anticipating the response to our singing but seeing ourselves creating each moment of the performance. The response, in any case, is always out of our control.

Three Elements of Positive Visualization

We should visualize three things before a performance. First, we visualize the physical atmosphere of the audition space. If we have been there before, we can actually imagine the contours of the room, see ourselves walking into that room dressed to the nines, smiling with confidence (but not over-the-top enthusiasm or gushiness), and announcing our first selection.

Second, we visualize each aria or song we might be asked to sing. We begin by thinking through the text of the piece, speaking it as if we are just conversing with someone directly, separate from the music. We think about what we want to communicate or express through this piece, what it means to us personally.

Third, we sing through the piece mentally, thinking about how the piece feels when our voice is truly free. We think through each syllable and pitch, imagining how they will feel when we are singing at our best. If we have visualized all of these things in advance, we are free to simply tell the story when the audition comes.

Audition Pet Peeves

Having sat through many auditions, I have developed two major pet peeves when listening to people sing. The first is for a singer to come in with over-the-top energy and enthusiasm, which comes across as pushy, in-your-face aggressiveness. If a singer is naturally a very upbeat, positive, and happy person, then that is exactly what I want him or her to be in an audition; however, often the singer is compensating for a lack of confidence by overdoing the friendliness factor, which comes across as insincere.

The opposite of that attitude is my other pet peeve—the apologetic audition. These people walk into the room and everything about them—their posture, gait, appearance, tone of voice, and facial expression—all communicate an apology. They are apologizing for taking my time, for not being technically perfect, for not having great high notes, whatever. Their singing usually sounds like an apology as well. They transmit no positive energy and in fact drain energy out of the listener.

These are extremes on opposite sides of the spectrum, but both are self-absorbed, needy, and obnoxious, and they give the listener nothing through their performance. The key is to find a balance between these two. As I discussed in A Balancing Act, we should try to find balance in every aspect of life. Of course, we need to be positive and upbeat, but we can do that and still be genuine and sincere. We can also be humble and confident, without apologizing for ourselves with every physical gesture or note we sing. We should never apologize, no matter where we are personally or professionally. Where we are at any given moment is where we are. We have worked hard to get to that point, and we must claim all the good things we have gained without apologizing for every weakness or failure.

If I had to pick one of these extremes as less offensive, I would say it is better to err on the side of more positive energy. I definitely prefer singers who come in overconfident, who believe they have something to offer and are proud of that, over someone who comes in apologetic for everything. An important idea to remember is that the audition begins the moment we walk into the room, and we must project an air of security and positive energy from that very first moment, without being in-your-face and obnoxious.

> The best singing in an audition or performance is when the singer has come to the stage with nothing to prove. This has to do with the discipline of intention. In singing one must surrender thinking about singing and create in the moment. That is the creation of continual expression, surrendering to the music and character as completely as possible during performance.
>
> Christine Armistead, soprano

"Have Church!"

Once we have the "grill warmed up" and we have gone through all the steps of positive visualization, then, as my Southern baritone student says, "You gotta have church!" In other words, when it is our time to perform, we just go on stage and give our all. We sell the piece, not apologizing for anything, not wishing we were someone else or had a different voice. To "have church" means we go out there thinking, "I'm here and I'm going to give you everything I've got." We follow through on all the positive energy we gained through the visualization process, and that energy can sometimes carry us even beyond what we think we are capable of technically and vocally.

A common mistake is to think of auditions as auditions, meaning that we hope the audition panel likes us and gives us the job. That attitude wastes energy for something over which we have absolutely no control. Instead, think of every audition as a performance opportunity, the chance to use your unique gifts and personal experiences to tell a story. Granted, audition panels are usually much more jaded than the general public, so they can be more difficult to touch, but we should take that as a challenge and commit to delivering everything we've got to the very best of our ability, to communicate something special. Any time we sing for other people, we've got to "have church!"

A Five-Step Process for Learning Repertoire

The process by which we learn repertoire is crucial in communicating the message of the piece. It is also crucial to learn repertoire in such a way that we don't develop bad habits or "baggage" along the way. I present the following five-step process for learning repertoire. Those who have followed these steps generally testify to learning the piece more securely and with more vocal freedom.

Step One: Study the Text

All great vocal music begins as text, so that is where we should begin when learning it. If the text is in a language other than our native language, we should first write out a word-for-word translation on the music so that when we are working on the piece in practice or in lessons, both we and our teacher or coach know that we know what the words mean and, if there is a word the coach or teacher doesn't know, it will be written on the page. However, just having the text written in the score doesn't mean we know what it is about, so after this translation, we add a phrase-by-phrase translation so that we have a basic idea of what the words are trying to communicate.

We should not skip this step just because the text is in our native language. When I started singing, I was not a good interpreter of poetry, even in English. I knew what all the words meant, but I didn't really know what the poet was trying to say. Most songs are poems, however, so we must develop the ability to understand what a poem is trying to say. Because of my musical orientation, I learned to interpret poetry from the great *Lieder* composers. When I knew the meaning of all the words and then listened to Schubert's, Schumann's, and Brahms's musical interpretations of those poems, I came to understand what the poem was about, at least from that particular composer's point of view. Although we may study the text of a song and know its meaning, we shouldn't make final decisions about our own interpretation of that text until we become familiar with the composer's interpretation.

Step Two: Speak the Text

We should be able to speak the text of an aria or song as if we were going to perform a dramatic reading of that text in its original language. Obviously, to do this, we must know the meaning of all the words and our diction must be correct (including IPA notation and coaching with diction experts). To get the feeling of the voice buzzing as in Simply Speaking Simply, it is helpful to also speak the text in a steady but energized monotone. Listen to Audio Sample 30 for a demonstration.

 AUDIO SAMPLE 30: Speaking the Text in Monotone

Next, I recommend that singers speak a literal translation of a phrase of the text in their native language, then immediately speak that phrase in the original language. This practice develops a connection between the words and their literal meaning. Listen to Audio Sample 31 for a demonstration.

 AUDIO SAMPLE 31: Phrase-by-Phrase Translation

Ultimately we want to feel that when we are singing we are not translating the language but actually speaking in it. Once we have all of that well in hand, we speak the text as if in a dramatic reading, with the flow, syntax and emphasis of the original language. It takes an intense amount of study and preparation, but it makes a huge difference in the end. Listen to Audio Sample 32 for a demonstration.

 AUDIO SAMPLE 32: Speaking the Text as a Dramatic Reading

Step Three: Speak the Text in Rhythm

This step is the first time we look at the music, and even now, we only look at the rhythm. The beginning stages will seem dry and boring—simply speaking the text in monotone but with strict attention to the rhythm. Obviously, we may need to mark the beats in the music to be certain that we are learning the rhythms correctly. We keep rhythm by conducting and/or tapping the beats, and in doing so we learn where the stress falls in the language and how that corresponds with the pulse, rhythm, and meter of the music. The phrases should not sound punchy, like we are whacking the beats, but we still maintain the correct rhythm. Singers must learn to generate their own internal pulse of the music and always speak and sing the text in connection to that pulse. If we don't generate our own pulse, we won't be able to maintain free-flowing air, so knowing the rhythm is essential to good technique. Ultimately, we want to be able to speak the text in rhythm, with legato and flow.

Step Four: Get the Pitches in Your Ear

A singer cannot approximate pitch without hearing it first. To hear before the sound happens is called *audiation*. Audiation results in us never guessing at a pitch before we attempt to sing it. Therefore, we must get the pitches in our ear. By far, the best way to accomplish this is to play the pitches ourselves at the piano. Singers who have limited piano skills must develop enough skills to play their own pitches at the piano.

Playing our own pitches at the piano combines the senses of touch, sight, and sound. We then feel, see, and hear the pitches, rhythms, and the intervals (distance between the pitches). Doing this gives us a more complete audiation experience.

Once we can play our pitches at the piano, we then speak the text on a plain monotone while playing the pitches. This underscores the constant creation of phonation and legato line while securing the pitches in our ear.

Singers typically think only of getting the vocal line in their heads; however, it is crucial to also learn the surrounding pitches—the environment in which our vocal line happens (i.e., the accompaniment). I recommend that if they have the piano skills singers should play their own accompaniment to hear the surrounding pitches. (I don't recommending singing *while* playing the accompaniment because we are not paying enough attention to our singing for it to be free.) Playing the accompaniment ourselves gives a much deeper comprehension of the piece than we can get just by looking at it or hearing it when someone else plays. When we actually feel the chords in our hands and sense the harmonic progression, the piece more naturally becomes our own. Feeling the chords also deepens our tactile, visual, and aural experience of the piece. Those singers who don't have the piano skills to play their own accompaniment should hire (or persuade) a pianist to record it for them.

If the piece we are learning is with orchestra, then we should get a recording to hear what the orchestration sounds like. However, I want to emphasize that it is never a good idea to learn pitches by listening to recordings. Learning a piece from a recording leads to poor musicianship because we are not generating the music ourselves. Also, the best singers on the best recordings occasionally make mistakes in rhythm, pitch, pronunciation, and technique. Listening to a recording of a piece tends to make singers imitate what they hear, thus potentially leading them to learn some mistakes. *After* they have completely learned the piece on their own, I strongly recommend that singers listen to as many recordings of the piece as possible to hear different interpretations and broaden their own spectrum of interpretive choices.

Even if we are fabulous sight-readers or have perfect pitch, I still recommend playing the pitches ourselves at the piano. Our goal is to get to the point where there is no more guessing about text, rhythm, or pitch so that when all of those things are securely in place, we can move to the final step of this process.

Step Five: Sing It

The final step in learning a piece is to sing it. This five-step process can be tedious and frustrating because singers typically want to immediately open the music and sing it to hear how it sounds and feels in their voice. As a singer, I am sympathetic with that desire, so one way to speed up the process is to work on one phrase at a time through all five steps. It is not necessary to do an entire role one step at a time, but if we come upon a difficult phrase that we know will be particularly challenging, we should start with that phrase and go through all five steps on it.

When learning an entire role, we might want to start with the arias first, or start with the recitatives and then do the arias. However we do it, it is important to learn a piece using all five steps of this process. This way, when we begin to sing, we are not guessing at any pitches and we don't have any baggage to strip away. We can sing the piece the very first time with a free technique, having programmed in all the rhythmic, textual, and musical details beforehand. Also, starting with the text first (i.e., speaking), and then adding pitches and rhythms (i.e., airflow), we learn the piece in a way that generates flow and balance in the voice.

REHEARSING A ROLE, OR WHEN TO MARK

The rehearsal process deserves special attention, and one of the most important considerations in rehearsing is knowing when to *mark*. In classical singing, marking refers to singing without the full voice.

The first and most important point about marking: If you cannot mark freely, you should never do it. In fact, it is better to sing fully all the time if you don't know how to mark freely. Some people's version of marking is singing very tight and soft, which has no value. Healthy marking is singing everything on a falsetto sigh, in which the air flows freely without engaging the cords. When marking this way, we still articulate all the vowels to encourage airflow as we would in full singing. Another way to mark is to speak the role in an easy range, an octave lower than the actual pitches.

The purpose of marking is to preserve the voice in rehearsal, but we should not develop bad habits in the process. The best time to mark is during staging rehearsals when we are doing all the dramatic work. We should not fully sing the dramatic sections until we start going through whole scenes at a time. The ability to do this well depends on how much preparation we have done before arriving at the first rehearsal. If we haven't learned all the music thoroughly, we might have to sing through several rehearsals without marking, just to get the role in the voice. And if we have limited rehearsal time, we may have to sing a lot of the staging rehearsals anyway. Generally, there is enough rehearsal time that we can mark during staging rehearsals, so we should mark as much as possible, but always in a healthy way to avoid tension while engaging in the drama.

In musical rehearsals, which are usually separate from staging rehearsals, we should sing fully through everything, without acting. We should focus on all the musical aspects and sing with a free technique, but stay as detached as possible from the drama. If we keep these two tracks separate, then join them when we get to whole scenes and run-throughs, we might avoid developing a lot of vocal baggage from trying to be dramatic before we get the role in the voice.

When I was teaching in Houston, a famous dramatic soprano came to sing the title role of Strauss's *Elektra*, which she had performed many times all over the world. I noticed that she never sang with her full voice until the first dress rehearsal, but during all the staging rehearsals she marked and was fully engaged in the drama. When she finally did sing in the dress rehearsal, she was spectacular—so amazing, in fact, that I went back and saw the production three times.

SINGERS ARE ACTORS

Actors normally internalize drama so that they genuinely feel the emotion of the character they are portraying. Often their bodies respond to that emotion with muscular tension. This kind of muscular tension can inhibit the airflow and the free vibration of the singing voice. For the singer, the voice is the principal medium of communication. If we want the audience to feel what we are communicating, we can't feel the emotion and its corresponding muscular tension in the way actors often do. Singers function more as a vessel for the drama than a participant in it. If we felt emotions on stage the way we experience emotion in everyday life, our voices would become very tight. And if the voice is tight, we can't communicate completely. While singing, we *convey the intentions* rather than *feel the emotions* because feeling genuine emotion can bind the voice. If the voice is free, we will not feel the musculature of the body that is often engaged in dramatic acting.

Having said that, I want to clarify that I don't think a free voice excuses singers from having to act. The "park-and-bark" approach to opera has always been offensive to me because there is an assumption that impressive sounds are all that is needed. But classical singing is a different art form than straight stage acting. To reiterate, the voice is our primary medium of expression, followed by the face and the body. But in singing, if the voice is not free, our facial expressions and body language are not really effective. It is a hierarchical issue: We want the face and the body to be communicative but not entangle the voice.

The real key to acting for singers is simply *to mean what we say when we say it*. We don't need to indicate the meaning through overly dramatic gestures or facial expressions—we simply mean what we say and let the voice, face, and body communicate with sincerity. Just as bad actors sometimes try to indicate meaning through awkward gestures, singers often try to indicate the meaning by "coloring" the sound of a certain word. If we sing freely and mean what we say, the words will have all the color they need on their own.

For example, you have surely had the experience of being in a terrible mood when your mother calls on the telephone. If you try to answer with a cheerful "hello," she immediately asks, "What's wrong?" She hears the bad mood in your voice, even though you are indicating a different tone. I don't think singers intentionally disguise what they are feeling, but that's what they are doing when they indicate the meaning, just like trying to have a cheerful voice when answering the phone. When the voice is functioning freely, the listeners will hear what we truly mean.

This idea assumes, of course, that we actually know what we are saying. Unfortunately, many singers feel that their technique or voice quality is all they need to be concerned with. I recommend that singers do all the research an actor would do in preparing a role: Study the source material for the opera—read background information, historical context, commentaries, and studies about the opera and their character so that they "get under the skin" of the character. All of those things inform the performance, but once we get in performance, we have to leave behind all the research we have done and just communicate. All of the time spent learning the meaning of each word and researching the background of the opera is essential, but when we get on stage to perform, we have to stop thinking about all of it and just mean what we say. Then, we make sure that the face and the body are enhancing (not distracting from) the meaning that we are communicating through the voice.

WHAT TO DO ON PERFORMANCE DAY

Performance day behavior and activities are very personal things and will be different for every singer. The important task is to find out what we need to do on performance day to be able to give our best performance and then do that. When I was an apprentice at Des Moines Metro Opera, I wanted to see my colleagues perform their scenes. Therefore, I sat in the audience during the performances. When my scene was coming up, I would go backstage and get ready to perform. Most of my colleagues, on the other hand, were backstage the whole time, vocalizing, wrapping their necks in warm towels, or doing whatever they needed to get ready to perform. Everyone has different needs.

I always had an educational bent; I was curious about other people's performances, so I liked to watch what they did. That did not hurt the effectiveness of my own performance—I was prepared and knew what I needed to do to be ready for a good performance. Later, when I became a teacher, I found that it was not a good idea to perform after a full day of teaching. There is value in having the performance day to focus and relax, but exactly what we do to focus or relax will vary from person to person.

I once visited Annette Daniels, a mezzo-soprano student of mine who was singing Charlotte in *Werther* at Chatauqua Opera, and on the day of the performance I went to the grocery store with her. She bought some junk food, a soft drink and sports drink, and then she said, "Of course, I also have to buy lemon and honey." I laughed, and said, "Well you do whatever you need." She asked, "Don't you think lemon and honey help?" I told her that the acidity in the lemon helps eliminate the feeling of phlegm in the throat and the honey going down slowly feels like it coats the throat; however, they have no direct impact on the vocal folds because they bypass them on their descent through the digestive tract. But if drinking lemon and honey made her feel better, then she should definitely do it. The things we do to prepare for a performance will vary from person to person, but it is important to keep a healthy psychological perspective and not come to regard lemon and honey as a magic potion for creating a perfect performance.

Warming Up before a Performance

The exercises we learn in the Inventions are not intended as warm-ups before a performance. They are a routine that conditions us to "play the game"—sing. Just as an elite athlete has a daily exercise regimen to stay conditioned in the off-season and on nongame days, the Inventions offer an exercise routine to condition and maintain the voice on nonperformance days. On game day, athletes would never do a full-out exercise regimen because it would tire their body, and they would not give their best in the game. Likewise, if done immediately before a performance, the Inventions can tire the voice and use energy that is best saved for the performance. Singers are elite athletes—we just don't think of ourselves in that way.

Warm-ups are what we do to stretch and get the muscles limber and loose. The best warm-up for singing is to do the sigh exercise, Free-Flowing Air. That Invention stretches the vocal folds healthily by using the breath and vibrating the edges of the folds without actually engaging the vocalis muscles. Additionally, we are also getting the air to move and opening up our resonators. The Wobble exercise could also be helpful because it is primarily an airflow exercise, but it does require the vocal folds to respond. We should be wary of doing the full regimen of the Inventions before a performance. If we have been talking all day before a performance, we will probably be pretty warmed up already and will need little if any warm-up.

Different Inventions have helped me more than others at different points in my singing career, depending on what I need to work on most at the time. If I'm experiencing jaw tension, I use Spontaneous Combustion. If I'm finding that my voice is feeling or sounding out of focus, I use Simply Speaking Simply. If I'm feeling like my high notes are hitting a 'ceiling' I use Getting High to access the higher registers. If I'm not getting the colors and overtones that make the sound 'special,' I do Free-Flowing Air. If I catch myself trying to put my voice into place, I will use The Wobble to keep my voice loose and agile. It's hard to say which exercise helps me the most, but if I had to choose a favorite, it would be Spontaneous Combustion. If I have very little time to warm up, I will use that exercise. It incorporates Simply Speaking Simply and Free-Flowing Air and I can hear immediately if I'm doing both of those well.

Jennifer Moore Poretta, soprano

Much of our success as singers depends on our personal management skills. As with performance day habits, everyone's style of personal management will be different. I have students who can study a musical score for an hour and have it completely memorized and others who require months of repetition and study to accomplish this. Most of us fall somewhere between the two extremes. It is important to know how much time we need to memorize music and then organize our time so that we are prepared for rehearsals.

At Juilliard, I give my students very specific deadline requirements for memorization and very strict consequences if those deadlines are not met. All of my students are required to learn a certain amount of repertoire each semester. If by the eighth week of the semester, they can't sing at least half of that repertoire from memory, I fail them and drop them from the course. When students are preparing to give a recital, I require that they sing the entire program from memory a full month before the recital. If they can't do that, I cancel the recital. These are not arbitrary deadlines; I simply superimpose a pattern of personal organization so that when they are on their own as singers, they know how long it takes to memorize music and they experience how much more communication is possible in the actual performance when memorization is done well in advance.

Once singers are working professionally, they must know themselves well enough to know if they should accept several new roles in a given year. If it is not possible to learn all of those roles in a year, they shouldn't accept them. It all depends on one's own learning speed. For example, if you and I need to be at Carnegie Hall at 7 p.m., it doesn't matter if it takes me twenty minutes by foot and it takes you forty-five minutes by subway; the important thing is that we both arrive there on time. Likewise, it doesn't matter if the soprano singing Mimi in *La Bohème* requires two years to learn her role and the tenor singing Rodolfo can learn his role in a week as long as they both have their parts learned when rehearsals begin.

When I was singing the title role in *Falstaff* at the University of Houston, I intended to do lots of background research—read all the Shakespeare plays in which Falstaff is mentioned and learn the role first in Italian and then English (because we were performing it in English). However, I had not budgeted my time well and had only accomplished a small amount of this background work, which meant I had not spent much time even learning the notes and rhythms. Because I am a good sight-reader, I went to the first rehearsal after a full day of teaching and sang through the first couple of scenes without missing any pitches or rhythms. The coach therefore assumed that I had the piece learned well. She said, "Great! Let's start coaching it." I told her I was basically sight-reading and it would not be profitable to coach it at this time. The best use of my time would be to run it a couple more times so that I could get past the point of reading. I did not want to start coaching it until I really had the whole piece in my ear, voice, and body. It behooves us to organize our time so that we can come to all rehearsals with our roles thoroughly prepared.

Singers with great voices and solid technique sometimes lose work because they come to rehearsals unprepared. Even though they "pull it off" by performance time, these singers have so frustrated the opera company staff during the rehearsal period that the company is hesitant to hire them again. When I was at Houston, I witnessed singers being fired because they weren't prepared when they arrived for rehearsals. If we show up for rehearsals without having done our homework, it can have a detrimental effect on our career. The opera world is very small, and a reputation for being unprepared spreads quickly among the ranks.

After people have established their careers, their managers sometimes book more engagements than they are capable of preparing in time. We should know ourselves better than our managers do; we have to take care of ourselves first and foremost and be responsible to take only the amount of work we know we can prepare in time. We might have to turn down good offers and opportunities, even against the advice of managers and agents. But at the end of the day, if we are aware of our time management abilities, we are more likely to succeed at each job opportunity.

FINANCIAL MANAGEMENT

In addition to time management as a professional singer, we must learn to manage our financial lives as well. I have known fabulously talented artists who are incapable of taking care of themselves financially. Even though they are great artists and can always deliver when they get on stage, their financial lives are a mess, which severely affects the rehearsal process and increases performance anxiety.

Financial management is a common problem for singers. We artist-types are typically less structured and our income is less steady than that of people with nine-to-five jobs and steady salaries. Our tendency is to spend money when we have it. If we don't have money, then we go out and try to find more. Sometimes we will get a big chunk of money in May and then have no income until November, so we have to be much more disciplined and better planners than people who have a regular, steady income. If we are not capable of managing our finances ourselves, then we should get help from an accountant or financial planner to keep organized.

I have known singers who become emotionally crippled because they get into so much credit card debt that collection agencies and credit bureaus are constantly harassing them. That stressful situation hurts their ability to be artists. It is not because they don't make enough money—they simply don't know how to pace themselves and manage their finances well. People who need a steady income will probably not make it as singers because the income is sporadic and financial management requires much discipline and planning. We have to know how much money we need to make to pay our bills and taxes and plan for those in-between months when we have no work or income. If we get a check for $50,000 in February, we might be tempted to buy a new car. But if we don't have another gig lined up until December, we had better be prepared to live in that car if we decide to buy it. Financial management is very important to keep us happy and stress-free so that we have the energy and freedom of mind to focus on our art.

12

La Voce *Is You*

In the previous chapter I discussed the challenges involved in getting a career started, such as auditioning and choosing repertoire. In this chapter, I explore additional challenges singers face, including taking responsibility for their own careers and lives, professional etiquette and expectations, how to be a good colleague, how and when to say no, and dealing with conductors, directors, and colleagues. As in every other chapter of this book, the most important consideration in living life as a singer is always to be true to yourself.

TAKING RESPONSIBILITY

In contemporary society we have a tendency to blame others for anything that happens to us. It is much easier to play the victim than it is to "take the bull by the horns" and handle our own responsibilities. I try to help my students rid themselves of that tendency by insisting from the outset that they make their own decisions regarding their singing. I want them to gradually become independent of me, and the way they do so is by becoming more confident in their ability to make their own choices. They become more confident because I require them to make their own choices. I find that if students are expected to make their own decisions, they embrace that responsibility and settle into it.

It is common to resist taking responsibility for many of the decisions that I think singers should make, especially in the early stages of their careers. Choosing repertoire is one of the first important decisions to be made. I realize that choosing repertoire for students is one of the assumed tasks of a voice teacher. As I explained earlier, I rarely choose repertoire for my students because I feel it should be a personal choice. When younger singers have no idea how to choose repertoire, I send them to the library to listen to recordings, play through scores, and read translations. Through that process, they find music and texts they connect to personally. I give some parameters in which to make decisions, and if they still struggle to find repertoire, I will select five or six pieces for them to choose from, but I still refuse to make the final choice for them.

Students often ask my advice on whether to do a certain competition or sing a specific aria, and I do my best to present the pros and cons of each choice as I see it. That way, they may have more information on which to base their choice, but the choice is still ultimately theirs, and they leave the process empowered and more independent. Likewise, in teaching vocal technique, I give students instructions on what to do with the voice, but I can't force them to follow these instructions. They choose whether to follow my advice, and I leave that completely up to them. I can usually tell from week to week how much or how well they have practiced by hearing changes in their singing. If they are not improving, I just continue addressing the same issues, trying to find alternative ways to explain concepts until I hear improvement. I have been told that I am very patient because I keep waiting for improvement to happen. I don't think I'm patient at all, but I am relentless. Eventually, they get tired of my relentlessness and begin to take responsibility for changing their vocal production. Sometimes they even start practicing! At some point, they begin to see the results of applying the concepts, and they come to realize the cause and effect of working and improvement. In this way, I instill a sense of personal responsibility in my students for their own vocal technique.

Singers also have a tendency not to take responsibility for bad singing, blaming it on poor health or a bad mood. Almost without exception, within the first ten minutes of any lesson, singers give excuses about why they are going to sing poorly that day. It is subtle and unconscious that singers do it (I am guilty of it as well). The excuses include allergies or drainage or lack of sleep or "the voice just isn't working today." (My wife and I have joked about making a list of all the common disclaimers and posting it on the wall of the studio, so that when students walk in, they can just point to an excuse or check it off.) Students sometimes say *la voce* (the voice) is not working today, and I tell them, "Well, if *la voce* is not working today, it means *you* are not working today. After all, who is responsible for the working of *la voce*?" The only way we will ever learn to sing well is to take responsibility for *la voce* and do what it takes to make it work on any given day.

The voice is an organic, changing thing, and it might feel different every day. We should claim that ever-changing aspect of the voice, take responsibility regardless of how it feels on any given day, deal with it, and stop playing victim to external circumstances. Certainly bad things that impact our singing can and do happen to our voices, but when those things come along, we must face them with perspective and honesty. As a metaphor for life, taking responsibility for our singing helps us become more responsible people, which is a crucial step in becoming an adult and managing what are often complicated lives and careers.

Much of society seeks to stunt the maturation process, encouraging immaturity and dependence. Some parents think they are doing their children a favor by laying out their clothes each day and making all of their meals for them even into young adulthood. But they are actually doing them a disservice because their children never learn how to make their own meals or choose what to wear. Educational institutions are terribly guilty of this as well, telling students what to think and believe and how to act in every situation. I don't give my students parameters for life; rather, I give them behavioral guidelines for studying with me, including expectations and consequences (deadlines for memorizing music, cancellation policy, etc.). Following these guidelines helps set up a pattern of discipline and responsibility. Having communicated these expectations, I don't have to respond emotionally when they don't meet them. I simply hold them to the consequences of their actions. Of course, there sometimes are extenuating circumstances, but most of the time they "make their bed and have to sleep in it." This helps them to become responsible people.

To this day, my daughters sometimes tease me about always making them change their phrasing to take responsibility for their actions. For example, when they were little girls, if they spilled a glass of milk, they would say, "Daddy, the glass of milk fell over," but I would correct them and have them say, "Daddy, I knocked over the glass of milk." Fear of negative consequences often keeps us from claiming responsibility for our actions. However, we must consciously choose to become responsible in the face of so many entities that would absolve us of personal responsibility by seeking to make our choices for us. When singers enter the professional world, they encounter many people who are more than willing to tell them exactly what they should sing, how often they should be working, or even when to quit. We should never let agents, teachers, managers, conductors, coaches, or directors dictate how to live our lives or manage our careers. We should take their advice under consideration, but we are ultimately responsible for ourselves.

One of my students, a baritone, went through an interesting journey in this regard. He was raised in a very strict religion that told him exactly how to live his life, and he willingly complied with all of the expectations and rules set for him by his church, family, and community. In addition, before he began studying with me, he had worked with a voice teacher who had told him that the only way to have a successful career as a singer was to go to a top music school and get into a young artist program where he would get an agent and then begin working. That teacher also told him that if he was not working professionally by the age of thirty, he should try something else. He internalized this advice, and when things didn't turn out exactly as he had planned, he had a bit of a crisis. Meanwhile, his singing was improving, and he was starting to take full responsibility for his vocal life. That process helped him change the way he thought and behaved in his personal life as well. He let go of all the expectations imposed on him from external sources, thoughtfully considered what he truly wanted, and finally realized he wanted to focus on concert work as opposed to opera. It turned out concert music suited his voice and personality even better than opera, and he started getting more work than ever before.

The truth is that there are singers with respectable careers who never participated in a young artist program or earned a college education. There are no set patterns for establishing a singing career. We must discover who we are, what we are meant to be, and then work hard to stay on that path. Many people in the music business seem bent on wiping out individuality and uniqueness in singers—they want everyone to fit into a convenient and easily definable box, and they have the arrogance to tell people that their way is the only way to success. We must filter that advice, find our own path, and stay on it.

Just as we work hard to uncover the naked, essential core of our voice and then learn to sing with freedom and balance, we must employ a similar process in our personal and professional lives. Because singing is deeply connected to the rest of our lives, learning to sing with freedom and balance will likely contribute to more freedom and balance in life as well. When we accept responsibility for ourselves, we are willing to constantly reexamine and possibly change our idea of what we are meant to be. Like singing, life is created moment by moment. As we change, our career goals and priorities might change as well.

DEALING WITH DIRECTORS AND CONDUCTORS

In the opera world, conductors and directors have a great deal of authority over our creative output as singers. Though the music world is filled with many wonderful, generous, and talented conductors and directors, not all of them treat singers with respect, and they can manipulate others to meet their own needs. It is good to be sensitive to these people's needs and yet learn how to maintain personal and professional integrity while attempting to meet expectations. This can be like walking a tightrope. We must be careful not to let pride get in the way of accommodating their expectations. Often the demands on us are something as simple as an ornament or a particular phrasing of a vocal line. We might feel strongly about not doing what the conductor wants, but if the conductor is adamant, we should just swallow our pride and do what he or she wants. If it does not compromise our integrity or character to keep peace with the conductor, we should accommodate his or her desires and move on.

Singers should generally be open and flexible enough to try anything a conductor or director asks them to do. Those who are open and flexible are often the most well-liked and respected in the business. As a result, they are almost always working. If we know ourselves well and have the clarity to see what the conductor or director wants, we can almost always find a way to accommodate those desires. The very best conductors and directors are solicitous of singers' ideas, but there are many who are not, so we just have to be self-aware and able to stand up for ourselves when necessary. But instead of looking at our professional relationships as battles, it is better to look at them and think, "How can I make it so that this is a good experience for me and everyone else involved?"

However, if we are asked to do something that truly compromises our integrity or identity, we should find a tactful way to suggest an alternative. One of my mezzo-soprano students was singing a trouser role (where a woman portrays a boy or young man) at a major American opera house. She had a dark, chocolatey, rich sound, but both the conductor and director seemed to want a lighter, brighter voice in that role. They were constantly telling her to brighten her sound or "place it more forward." She worked hard to accommodate their wishes, but was vocally fatigued at the end of every rehearsal. During this rehearsal period, I worked with her to return to her own sound to maintain the freedom to sing the role, but they continued to ask for more brightness. It seemed they simply preferred a different type of voice in this role, and they were attempting to force her to produce the sound they desired. On my advice, she finally approached the conductor and director and expressed her frustration in attempting to produce the vocal timbre they wanted. Then she offered to bow out of the role so that they could find someone whose voice more closely matched their expectations. They immediately changed their tune and stopped harassing her about her sound. The key to her being able to negotiate that situation was that she knew herself and her own voice well enough to be able to make a difficult choice about singing that role. But she also gave it her best shot to accommodate their wishes and demands.

There is not always an easy solution to such situations, but seeking to always be true to yourself will be helpful in navigating them. Another one of my students was in a production in which the conductor had picked him as the "whipping boy," cruelly picking on him in front of the whole company. This particular conductor had made it a habit of choosing a scapegoat in each production. He would publicly humiliate this person to scare the entire cast into submission to his authority. My student was very frustrated because no matter how hard he worked, he was unable to please the conductor. Finally, he went to him in private and asked him to clarify what he was after. This student was an exemplary singer—an excellent musician, fabulous linguist, strong actor, and an incredibly sensitive performer. He was always thoroughly prepared and worked very hard, so there really was nothing to clarify. When confronted directly, the conductor just mumbled something about, "Well, you'll be just fine." After that, he stopped humiliating him in rehearsals.

In these cases, what seemed to be the issue was the conductor or director needing to establish authority, define territory, or feel worshipped by the singers. This kind of behavior often compromises the music making and the integrity of the production. When singers can tell that one of these things is the issue, they can swallow their pride and find ways to give the *impression* of being in submission, without compromising their character or identity. This often satisfies the unhealthy need for the conductor and/or director to manipulate and allows the true work of the art to go on.

How and When to Say No

The more success we have as singers, the more picky we can be about which jobs we will or won't take. As always, the most important thing in knowing which jobs to accept or turn down is knowing ourselves. We have to know ourselves well enough to know what will feel right—we have to do well by ourselves. A mezzo-soprano student of mine who has been working in Europe for several years told me she will no longer accept roles in productions where the musical values take a back seat to the production. Many people have said that the opera world is now "the director's world," meaning the director's concept for each production has taken priority over the music. In these cases, this mezzo-soprano says she can hardly enjoy creating the music. However, she had a long and successful European career because she found a way to meet the demands of the directors. Now that she has done that, she feels empowered to choose to leave it behind. Because she knows herself and what she wants out of her life and career, she knows when to say "no."

One of my soprano students works all over the world with great orchestras and opera companies. When she encounters a conductor who is ill prepared—doesn't know the meanings of the words or has not prepared the music—she tells her agent to add this conductor to the list of those she will not work with again. Her intent is not to be arrogant but to make great music, which is impossible with ill-prepared, incompetent conductors. Many people would counsel her against making this black list because it might limit her work opportunities. However, the opposite has actually happened. She now works only with the best conductors in the world—all of whom bring impeccable preparation, respect for singers, and tremendous knowledge of the repertoire to each performance. Therefore, each performance is rich and memorable, her work is universally respected, and her career is more rewarding.

These two singers knew when to say no because they felt their integrity was compromised by the production or conducting. There are other reasons to turn down professional singing opportunities. Those reasons include having too little time to prepare, feeling inadequate to the demands of the role, and simply not connecting to the character or the piece. The key to making these difficult decisions is knowing ourselves.

Preparedness: The Key to Being a Good Colleague

The most important part of being a good colleague is to come thoroughly prepared to the first rehearsal. It is appalling to me how often people come unprepared, even at the highest professional levels. Singers should always come to every rehearsal with their music securely learned and no legitimate excuse for anything less. If people are not able to learn a score on their own, they either need to go to school to acquire the skills to do so or hire a coach accompanist to help them learn it. The important thing is to do whatever is necessary to be ready for the first rehearsal.

Occasionally, very busy singers will accept an engagement without having adequate time to learn the role. In this scenario, it is wise to advise the company of this before arriving and ask for assistance to complete their preparation upon arrival or to offer to bow out so they can find a singer who already knows the role. Most companies will work with the singer to get the piece prepared in time. Either way, singers should take responsibility for the situation, and I would emphasize that this should be the *exception*, not the normal mode of operation.

I have sat in on behind-the-scenes discussions at opera companies where a singer's lack of preparedness is discussed, and it is a very serious concern. If the person being discussed is a superstar on whose reputation and fame the whole production depends, the lack of preparedness might be tolerated. But there are few people of that stature in this business, so it behooves all singers, especially young singers, to show up thoroughly prepared for every rehearsal.

Preparedness is the key to being a good colleague. If we are not prepared, the rest of the cast will have to sit around while we struggle through our pitches and rhythms and learn pronunciations. This displays a lack of responsibility and integrity and total disrespect for our colleagues. Every member of the production should show up equally prepared. If it is a world premiere and there are no past recordings to study, or if it is in a totally new language, we must know what it will take to get the piece learned and then take all the necessary steps to learn it. That usually means hiring a coach to help us prepare it. Hiring a coach to help us learn a new role is an investment in our career, and the expense should be a secondary consideration.

Some people are good enough musicians that they can look at a score while they are on the airplane traveling to an engagement and have it totally learned by the first rehearsal. I know others who require months of repetition and practice to learn music. The key is to know ourselves and what it takes to learn a piece. When we get on stage, nobody cares how long it took us to learn the piece. It may take me five times longer to learn an opera than it takes my colleagues, but the equalizing factor is that we all must have it completely learned by the first rehearsal, whatever it takes.

BE A GENEROUS COLLEAGUE

Once we have learned our music thoroughly, we must learn to work with people on a personal level. Because singers are generally outgoing people, this is not a big challenge; they often find people they click with in most productions. But there are other people who are more difficult. There are neurotic people in this business who constantly drain energy out of everyone around them, seeking affirmation for whatever insecurity they might be dealing with on any given day. One of my students calls them "drainful" people. Sometimes part of being a good colleague is allowing them to "drain" us for a short period of time. That doesn't mean we compromise our integrity or take responsibility for solving those people's problems, but we all need help from time to time. The key is to maintain our sense of integrity while helping them.

One of my students was hired for his professional debut in the role of Yamadori in Puccini's *Madama Butterfly* at a regional opera company. The person singing the role of Sharpless in that same production had been in the business for a while, and when he found out that my student was from his alma mater, he took him under his wing. At one point, the director was getting very frustrated with my student for not having a more "regal" bearing. The more experienced colleague thought that the reason the director was giving him such a hard time was that he was wearing jeans and a T-shirt to rehearsals. He suggested my student wear dress slacks and shirt to the next rehearsal. When my student repeated the scene with this change of attire, the director was very pleased and told him that he had finally acquired the appropriate regal bearing. I was very impressed that this experienced baritone would be so generous and collegial to my student.

This situation is a perfect example of being a generous colleague, while also showing the lengths to which we might need to go to meet the needs of the directors and conductors, as discussed earlier. With the help of his colleague, my student was able to read between the lines and figure out exactly what the director was looking for and then find a way to make him happy, even though he wasn't really changing anything about the way he played the role. He made a very positive impression in that production, and the company told him they would be looking for larger roles in which to engage him in the future.

A student of mine sang Adalgisa in a production of Bellini's *Norma* along-side a world-famous soprano who was scheduled to repeat that role at the Metropolitan Opera in the near future. During this production, they gained a great deal of respect for each other and enjoyed a collegial relationship. That soprano is sure to put in a good word for my student for the role of Adalgisa if the company is looking for someone to sing that role. In addition to coming to the first rehearsal prepared, being friendly, humble, and generous with our colleagues can be very important to career longevity.

DON'T MARK THE HERALD!

I once knew a singer who was performing the role of the Herald in Verdi's *Aida*. This role has only a few lines—he walks on stage, makes his pronouncement, and leaves. There was a day during rehearsals that his voice was not feeling well, so he marked his part. The conductor was livid. "Why are you marking this part?" he screamed. This singer got defensive and said, "Well, the tenor singing Radames is marking!" There is a huge difference between the demands of the two roles. Radames is an incredibly demanding role, so the tenor singing it had every right to mark his role in rehearsal. Additionally, the role of Radames was being sung by one of the world's most famous tenors, who had sung the role numerous times all over the world. But the young singer, just starting out in the business singing a small role in a major opera house, should always sing the *entire* part.

This is a matter of knowing who we are, where we are in our professional development, where we are going, what we want from our careers, and making choices based on those priorities. A young student singing the Herald is in a much different place than a superstar singer singing Radames in *Aida*, and that student should humbly accept his place and act accordingly. Much of the ability to do that is built over time as we better learn our strengths and weaknesses. Just as in the business world, if we sell ourselves short, we will always be short. If we oversell ourselves, no one will buy.

As a faculty member, I once sang a role in a student production with a conductor that I felt was incompetent. The audience seldom recognizes a conductor's competence, so if the conductor is not in sync with the singers, people assume the singers are off or don't know their parts—in short, the singers look bad. In this production the horn players were continually playing incorrect notes that the conductor was not fixing. So at the *sitzprobe* (a German word meaning "sitting rehearsal," for a musical read-through with orchestra and singers), I went to the offending horn players myself and corrected the pitches. It was difficult to sing the correct pitch when the accompanying chord was wrong. Even though the horn players didn't expect or want to hear this feedback from me, it was apparent the conductor was not aware of their errors. Because I was a faculty member, I felt I had the right to correct them myself. I was aware of my role in this process and could make choices accordingly.

There were many changes of meter and tempo in this opera, none of which would work without eye contact between the conductor and me. In rehearsal, he and I had agreed on how those changes would take place, but when the production was on stage and he was in the pit, he never made eye contact with me at any of those agreed-on places. I understood that he had to keep his head somewhat in the score to cue the student orchestra members and try to keep the music together. Even so, without making eye contact, all the singers were floundering. So before the final dress rehearsal, I had to confront him about this issue. We met privately, and I threatened to walk off the stage if he didn't get his head out of the stand at those crucial junctures. I am normally not comfortable taking that kind of confrontational stance, and certainly in most cases a singer cannot do that with a conductor. However, because I understood my position on the faculty and because of the crucial nature of my role in holding the opera together musically, I felt compelled to confront him. I am certainly not recommending this course of action; the point is that we must know our position in the business well enough to be able to make crucial decisions that can make or break a specific performance or even a career.

Many people feel that conductors or directors should make all of the decisions for them, but ideally every production is a collaboration among conductor, director, and singers. Singers should feel empowered to contribute to the process in meaningful ways, even if their input is not solicited. That said, if you are singing the Herald in *Aida*, you don't give your input—you just go on stage, sing, and get the job done. It takes humility and wisdom to determine where we fit in the business, and therefore when and how to give input.

13

Lifestyles of the Healthy Singer

The human voice is integral to all aspects of life—emotional, spiritual, psychological, intellectual, and physical. So when we uncover the naked voice, we uncover the naked self. A healthy singer is a healthy human being. Part of the Wholistic Approach to Singing is caring for the physical body, which not only encases the vocal folds but is a part of the singing instrument itself. Singers therefore have to pay even more attention to their health than most people because their identity and sometimes their livelihood depend on it.

Bookstores are brimming with books about how to improve one's emotional, spiritual, psychological, and intellectual health, so in this chapter I will focus mainly on the aspects of physical health that relate directly to the vocal instrument. The physical process of learning to execute the Inventions properly seems to spill over into all aspects of life, which is probably why so many of my students have told me how their lives have changed as a result of learning how to sing. In lessons, I try not to directly address the emotional, spiritual, or psychological aspects of singing, but because the process is so intimately connected to all aspects of life, learning how to sing inevitably has an impact on the whole person.

The first consideration for healthy singers is care of the vocal instrument, and one of the most important aspects of vocal health is to keep the vocal folds hydrated. The only way to do this is to keep the whole body hydrated. This means we continually take fluids into the body. I recommend water as an ideal fluid because many other fluids contain calories, caffeine, or alcohol, all of which can have negative effects on physical health. People can overdose on anything, and it is possible to drink too much water, but generally singers don't drink enough water. The only way to keep the voice lubricated and functioning well is to maintain a consistent high level of total body hydration.

Hydration enables the body to create the essential lubrication for the vocal folds to remain healthy despite heavy use. If we rub our hands together quickly, they heat up, and if we continue to rub them together for a long time, we eventually develop blisters. If those blisters are not allowed to heal, they become corns, which are hard bumps on the surface of the skin. However, if we put a lubricant like baby oil on our hands and rub them together, they take much longer to heat up. Likewise, if the vocal folds remain lubricated, they are less likely to become irritated and develop vocal fold pathology, such as nodules. When we sing or speak, the vocal folds flap against each other very quickly, and, as with the example of the hands rubbing together, they will heat up. If our body is not well hydrated, it is unable to create enough thin, clear mucus necessary to lubricate the cords. We are then more susceptible to vocal pathologies such as nodules—the vocal equivalent of corns. When the voice is dry, we press the vocal folds harder together, which can eventually damage the voice. This is the reason hydration is crucial to vocal health.

It is better to drink smaller amounts of water constantly throughout the day than to drink large amounts two or three times a day. The USDA recommends eight eight-ounce glasses of water per day, but if we drink caffeine or alcohol (which are diuretics and therefore eliminate fluid from the body), we must drink even more water. Also, if we are overweight, we must drink more water to compensate for the larger body mass (I have read that we should drink an extra glass of water for every twenty-five pounds we are overweight). The point in drinking all of this water is not to hydrate the vocal folds directly but to keep the *body* hydrated so that it can create the mucus that keeps the cords lubricated.

Many singers breathe in steam before a performance, which is helpful. Steam can coat the general area of the vocal folds with moisture, but it does not help produce mucus to lubricate the cords. If we are singing in an extremely high altitude or dry climate, steam can help compensate when our bodies are not up to the task of fully lubricating the cords, but this is a short-term solution.

Sometimes sickness causes congestion, which makes the body create thicker mucus, inhibiting vocal fold function. Some singers deal with this problem by flushing their system with warm, mild salt water to clear out congestion. A common approach to eliminate congestion is the use of antihistamines, but these drugs are the enemies of vocal hydration because they dry up excess mucus in the nasal cavities as well as the mucus on the vocal fold. This is often the only way for people to eliminate the congestion, but singers must understand that if they use antihistamines, they will need to compensate by drinking additional water. Dry mouth can result from lack of proper hydration, but it also can be a psychological or emotional response to nervousness or just the effect of breathing in dry air. In this case, many singers choose to use a lozenge or chewing gum to combat the feeling of dry mouth, but it should not be considered a substitute for hydration of the vocal folds.

Hydration, like vocal technique, is not a quick fix. We must discipline ourselves to get in the habit of consuming the proper amount of water throughout the day to keep our bodies constantly hydrated. One way to assess the body's level of hydration is to note the color of urine. The clearer it is, the more hydrated the body is. The catchphrase is "pee pale." Staying hydrated means that singers will normally drink more water than the average person. It also means we might have to visit the bathroom more often. (During this process, our bladders will become accustomed to holding more water and we won't always have this problem.) If that means having a water bottle attached to the hip, then so be it. Some singers are very particular about the brand of water bottle they carry around, refusing to drink from any but the most fashionable bottles! As long as they are drinking enough water throughout the day, I don't really care about the style of their water bottle. The bottom line is that hydration is one of most important considerations for vocal health.

SOME UNHEALTHY VOCAL HABITS

Hydration is the positive, proactive aspect of caring for the vocal instrument, but there are many things we should avoid. Anything that puts undue pressure on the vocal cords can be detrimental to the voice and has the potential to cause damage. I will discuss two typical types of vocal damage later in this chapter, but many of the more common vocal pathologies can be diagnosed as prenodular swellings, which means the area of irritation has not yet hardened into a nodule and may be corrected through vocal therapy.

Prenodular swelling usually has more to do with the way people use their voices in everyday life than how they use the voice in singing. Many people assume their singing technique is causing the prenodular swellings or nodules, but that is not normally the case. The most common form of vocal abuse is when people use their voice all day long and put unhealthy pressure on their vocal folds in the way they speak. For example, if someone works in a loud restaurant (the common lot of many singers in New York City), they have to scream to be heard, and an eight-hour shift of screaming will stress the voice. Broadcasters can get nodules when, in an attempt to sound authoritative and commanding, they press on the voice. Whispering can also strain the voice, and coughing or clearing the throat for a long time can cause damage. In certain cases, one hard cough can actually cause a polyp (more on that later). People whose voices are integral to their professional lives must take extra precautions and make careful plans to avoid bad vocal habits. That could mean avoiding smoky or loud bars and restaurants, not talking much during long road trips, and not speaking loudly when outside.

Another area of concern is drug use. I am not a pharmacist or doctor, but many medications (legal and otherwise) have a dehydrating effect on the voice. We should always be very careful when using any kind of chemical substance, and singers must take extra care to know which drugs might have a detrimental effect on the voice. Whenever we consider using any kind of drug, we should consult a physician to find out precisely what the potential vocal side effects may be. We need not be paranoid or oversensitive, just smart and balanced.

SMOKING

Smoking is the stupidest thing a singer can do. In the United States, we have come a long way in educating people about the disastrous effects of smoking, but for singers, it is not a moral issue or even primarily a health issue—smoking is simply antithetical to healthy singing because it sucks moisture out of the tissue it passes and negatively affects lung capacity. Smoke is dehydrated air, and even secondhand smoke can affect the voice. As smoke passes through the membranes of the mouth, the sinus cavities, the throat, the trachea (which includes the larynx), bronchial tubes, and lungs, it draws moisture out of the surrounding tissue. In doing so, it dehydrates those membranes that require moisture to function. The unhealthy dry lung tissue shrinks and is more susceptible to disease. The resultant dry vocal folds, as discussed in the hydration section, are more susceptible to damage because the membranes cannot consistently produce the essential lubricating mucus.

We have all heard stories about famous singers who smoke. I am not arguing that smoking will cause the voice to sound terrible; indeed, some singers smoke and still sing beautifully. However, we run an exponentially greater risk of vocal damage by smoking. Just listen to the speaking voice of a seventy-year-old woman who has smoked her entire life. Her voice has developed a low, raspy quality and a hack. If we want our voices to be healthy and last a long time, why would we ever do that? If I find out my students smoke, I strongly encourage them to quit. Although I understand the emotional hold any addiction can have, smoking may be the worst one for a singer.

DIET AND EXERCISE

Our bodies are our instruments, so singers should always eat a healthy diet and exercise regularly. We all know how to be healthier than we typically are, so there is no need to lay out a detailed diet and exercise program here. The challenge is actually finding a routine and settling into it consistently. Depending on our lifestyle and habits, settling into a routine can be a big challenge. When I am significantly overweight, it is much more difficult for me to move around and exercise, but when I am thinner, exercise becomes much more enjoyable—it is a self-perpetuating cycle.

Fad diets and nutrition guides abound, but a commonsense diet means not consuming too many calories yet getting enough calories so that the body feels energized and nourished. As with every other aspect of this process, it is about balance. We should integrate our desire for balanced, free singing with a healthy lifestyle that includes regular exercise and a balanced, nutritious diet.

Few singers are obsessive exercisers, so almost all of us need to exercise more than we actually do. I am a proponent of all kinds of exercise, including resistance training, because it increases lean muscle-to-fat ratio, speeds up the metabolism, and encourages proper diet, which provides more energy and thus more desire to exercise. However, when doing resistance training, we should never overadduct the glottis, squeeze the cords together, or put subglottal pressure on the cords (which causes the grunting sounds heard often in gyms). That action will overdevelop the adductor muscles, which for singing do not need to be strong; in fact, we try to loosen and relax the adductor muscles for good singing. For serious body builders, this can be a significant problem because it is practically impossible to lift a lot of weight even with few repetitions and not overadduct the vocal folds. The best option is to use less weight but more repetitions, which allows us to build muscle without damaging the voice. The rate of muscle gain might not be as rapid, but we conserve our voices in the process. In resistance training, we should exhale during exertion, keeping the glottis open.

In addition to resistance training, aerobic exercise is great for singers because when doing aerobic exercise we focus on breathing consistently in and out, letting the air flow and fill the lungs with oxygen. Many singers find a gym wherever they travel. Others develop exercise programs they can do in their hotel rooms. We should find what works for us, what we need to stay healthy and strong, and then discipline ourselves to incorporate those things into our lives.

PHYSICAL APPEARANCE

Opera is now sold to the mass market through television. Opera in the United States is different from that in Europe, where it is an integral part of the cultural life of most cities, big and small. Europeans often understand the history and priorities of opera, specifically, that the appearance of the singers is not as important as the quality of their voices to convey the drama. Outside of Europe, companies have recently tried to make opera accessible to a larger audience through televised performances with subtitles. Most of society today is used to seeing thin, beautiful people on television and in movies. We expect the same thing in opera, particularly televised opera. Therefore, it is much more difficult for a plus-size soprano to pull off a believable Violetta (in Verdi's *La Traviata*), dying of consumption, than it might have been before the advent of televised opera. Less opera-savvy audiences today expect visual realism, which means the characters on stage often have to look the part as well as sound the part.

Opera companies seem to be competing for an increasingly diverse audience, which includes the non–opera-savvy, so they are naturally casting more beautiful, youthful people. More established opera companies still place a high premium on vocal quality, even if the singers don't look physically like the characters they are playing. However, companies that are primarily dependent on ticket sales tend to put a higher premium on physical appearance. And some of the most established opera companies seem to be leaning that way as well. Most opera aficionados are familiar with the highly publicized firing of world-famous soprano Deborah Voigt from the Covent Garden production of Strauss's *Ariadne auf Naxos*—one of her signature roles. The alleged reason for her firing was that she was not able to fit into the "little black dress" that was part of the director's concept of the title character. At the highest levels, appearance is normally less important than the voice, but it is becoming more of an issue all the time.

Physical attractiveness can be an advantage for anyone. However, in the entertainment business (which includes opera), appearance has become much more important in recent years, so it behooves singers to be conscious of their appearance. I have mixed feelings about this. On one hand, physical health contributes to emotional, psychological, and vocal health, so we are well advised to pursue physical health. On the other hand, obsessing about our appearance can be just as unhealthy as being physically unfit. It is a shame that physical appearance should have priority over the use of the voice to portray the drama of a piece. It is especially upsetting when singers feel forced to resort to drastic measures to fit the look of a certain role, or a director's concept of that role.

It is important that people are healthy and feel good about themselves, whether or not they fit society's concept of attractiveness, which is always in a state of flux. Everyone is attractive to someone. The most important thing is that people pursue good health, accept and claim who they are, and embrace their uniqueness, which includes their physical appearance. Singing is intertwined with our emotional, psychological, physical, and spiritual health; and appearance in many cases, impacts that health. So for personal and professional reasons, singers should strive to be as healthy as possible and to look as good as possible. How we feel about ourselves should not be based on society's definition of attractiveness. Physical appearance is how people perceive us, and character is who we really are.

Everyone is familiar with the phrase, "It ain't over 'til the fat lady sings." Yet the stereotypical fat opera singer is a rarity these days. Many singers today are physically attractive. But an attractive person who is unable to convey the drama through the voice simply is not up to the task of singing opera. As with everything else in life, we should pursue a balance between appearance and the ability to communicate with the voice.

Bariatric Surgery

There has been a lot of attention paid to Deborah Voigt's weight since the Covent Garden "black dress" incident. She recently gave interviews to the *New York Times* about having gone through gastric bypass surgery to lose weight. This is a serious issue for overweight singers and something that requires much careful thought and consideration.

Overweight singers often seem to have beautiful and free high notes. As we explained in the breathing chapter, all singers are taught to expand in their abdominal area as they inhale. However, singers who carry weight around their abdomen seem to have an advantage in exhaling, because the weight of the fat around the abdomen encourages a release of the abdominal muscles, allowing a more steady, unencumbered ascent of the diaphragm. This is a simple product of the law of gravity. This means heavy singers can still be releasing "all their air, all the time," but the diaphragm will ascend more slowly and steadily, without any effort on their part to manage their exhalation. When people lose a great deal of weight, this advantage is eliminated. A skinny singer will definitely need more technical skill to balance airflow and phonation than a heavier singer.

If one loses a great deal of weight, the sensations of singing will be very different than when one was overweight. I know this from personal experience because I have lost (and gained) over 100 pounds four times in my life, and I felt a dramatic difference in my breathing after losing the weight. My high notes were much easier when I was overweight because of the exhalation advantage just described. But my low notes were not as clear because the same phenomenon caused me to expel too much air through relaxed cords. After losing a lot of weight, we cannot expect the body to expel air with the same ease as it did before. The common tendency is for people who have lost a lot of weight to press harder on the voice, forcing it to create the same kinds of sounds they created easily when they were overweight. The strain from that increased localized effort can cause significant damage.

I was once acquainted with a singer who was extremely overweight and had one of the most beautiful voices I had ever heard, particularly at the top of her range. After a period of time of not seeing her, I ran into her and did not recognize her even after she said hello. She had to tell me who she was because she had had bariatric surgery that caused her to lose 225 pounds. She seemed happy and looked svelte, gorgeous, and sexy—like a completely different person. About a year after she lost the weight, she began to have serious vocal problems. She had not been aware of the need to retrain to breathe with her new body; she had tried to compensate for the difference by pressing on her voice to make the same kinds of sounds she made before the weight loss. About this time, she came to me for a consultation lesson. I could tell from her speaking voice and then from her singing that she had serious vocal issues. Her voice was very hoarse and seemed incapable of phonating through much of the middle range.

My intention is not to dissuade people from considering bariatric surgery. I only want to emphasize that singers who decide to have it must retrain to sing with their new body or they risk serious vocal damage. I encourage weight loss, but we must adjust our breathing to accommodate a different body after losing weight. Although the basic principles of breathing are the same for all, different body types experience breathing differently, and when our body type changes, we must be aware of the differences.

In my experience, the two most common vocal pathologies are nodules and polyps. Nodules are hard bumps that usually form directly across from each other on the edges of the vocal folds. They begin to form when the cords become irritated and swell. Something like blisters form at the point of irritation, and if not treated, they can harden into a callus-like nodule. Nodules stick out in the middle of the cords so the folds are unable to adduct cleanly. The resultant sound in that place is breathy or nonexistent. To compensate for that "hole" in the sound, singers press the cords tighter around the nodules, which only exacerbates the problem.

Nodules almost always indicate a habitual, repeated misuse of the voice, not a single incident; if caught soon enough, they are often treatable or curable without surgery. Most voice professionals nowadays do not recommend surgery to remove nodules. In past decades, nodules were commonly surgically excised, but if the patients didn't change the way they used their voice, the nodules recurred, often on top of scar tissue from the previous surgery. Voice professionals suspect nodules when singers are habitually hoarse or their voice cuts out completely in a specific range. A program of vocal therapy is then prescribed to change their voice use. Therapy is much more effective before the swellings harden into actual nodules, but even after nodules form, therapy should be the first course of action.

I have found that some aspects of the Inventions, as described in Part II of this book, are useful as therapy when recovering from vocal nodules. Nodules result from pressing the cords together too hard, so anything that helps bring the cords together without pressing will help reverse damage from bad habits. Simply Speaking Simply and Spontaneous Combustion are not suggested in treating nodules because they are meant to bring the cords together with clean intensity, and people with nodules must press the cords together to get a clean sound. However, Free-Flowing Air and The Wobble—which focus on bringing the cords together with looseness and flexibility to allow the air to flow through freely—can be very therapeutic and helpful in the recovery process.

Although nodules can develop from poor singing technique, they more frequently develop from poor speech habits in everyday life (see Figure 13.1). In the early era of speech therapy, because nodules often resulted from pushing down the larynx to produce a lower speaking voice, patients were counseled to speak at a higher pitch level to reverse the negative effects. However, we can speak at a higher pitch and still put pressure on the voice. The best therapy for nodules is to do exercises that keep the cords from pressing together and yet help restore flexibility—like the sigh exercise in Free-Flowing Air. When

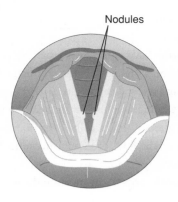

FIGURE 13.1. Vocal nodules

patients with vocal nodules recalibrate the way they use their voice, the nodules can fully heal and healthy vocalism can resume.

The second most common vocal pathology is the polyp. A polyp usually occurs when people cough extremely hard or put huge amounts of pressure on the voice, causing a rupture in the outer membrane of the vocal folds. The ruptured piece of tissue falls down between the vocal folds and creates a gravelly sound in a specific area of the voice. Usually singers can recall the specific moment when the polyp forms because they feel something happen while straining unusually hard for a high note or when coughing or clearing the throat.

Different from nodules, a polyp seldom heals from therapy and must be surgically removed (see Figure 13.2). In the hands of a highly specialized voice

FIGURE 13.2. Vocal polyp

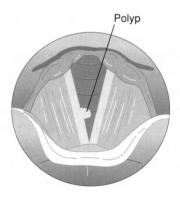

surgeon with modern surgical techniques, the danger of this procedure is minimal. When done correctly, normal vocal function can be resumed soon after surgery. However, I caution any singer to seek out the very best and most highly qualified surgeon they can find to do this procedure.

A good way to diagnose whether a singer has nodules or a polyp is for singers to do the siren phase of Free-Flowing Air. In the case of nodules, the voice will completely cut out consistently on one note or in a specific range. With a polyp, the voice will just get gravelly in one area, but normally won't cut out completely. If singers suspect that they might have nodules or a polyp, they should immediately seek the help of a medical voice professional for treatment and analysis.

WHEN SINGERS GET SICK

Recently, one of my students was scheduled to perform three songs in a recital. He got a cold and lost his voice the day before the performance, so he was being very careful and marking during his rehearsals, against the wishes of his coaches, who wanted him to sing fully despite the cold. Fortunately, he had developed enough technique that he sounded great, even when his voice wasn't 100 percent healthy. I partially agreed with the coaches wanting him to just sing, but I also acknowledged that he knew his voice better than I did. To get the same sense of balance in the sound that he got on healthy days, he had to push, which is never good. Normally, he was a very savvy performer, and on stage he could forget about technique and just sing. But when he was sick, he had to focus much more on airflow and clear phonation, keeping the vocal cords free, loose, and flexible, consciously choosing not to push. He wasn't able to be as free in his performance style as he normally would be, but everyone at the recital thought he sounded fantastic, despite being sick.

This is a tricky issue for singers. If we tell people we are sick, but we don't sound sick, they may think we are high-maintenance divas or wimps. We might even develop a reputation for being neurotic and undependable. On the other hand, if we are sick and we blow out our voices by overcompensating, we might get a reputation for being terrible singers. We must know ourselves and our voices well enough so that if we are sick, and we need to not sing for a while, we can do so with integrity. Or, if we are sick but have enough dependable technique to sing through it, we can go on with a performance anyway.

When our voice is thicker or drier than normal because of a cold, we have less margin of error and must concentrate more than we usually do on technical issues. I find that the more singers understand their technique and know their voice, the better they are able to deal with and sing through a sickness that affects the vocal cords. Focusing more intensely on technique in performance is not as fun as just letting go and singing, but we have to do it sometimes to be able to sing through sickness.

People with poor technique who get sick probably should cancel performances because they won't be able to cope with the illness. Those with a very good, strong, and healthy technique won't need to cancel as often because they are able to manage their voices despite unhealthy physical conditions. Singers who have solid technique know themselves and their voices well enough to know if they should cancel a performance or not. Generally, if singers are not running a fever or suffering from a serious vocal infection, they should be able to go on in a performance. If they are approaching a very prestigious opportunity that could make or break their career or take it to the next level and they get sick, they must weigh the pros and cons of going on despite not being at 100 percent. If the engagement is with a large, prestigious opera house, perhaps there is too much at stake to risk a technically weak performance.

However, if there is no cover or understudy and they have to go on anyway, some singers take doctor-prescribed steroids to help lessen the swelling in the voice. Steroids are a dangerous solution. Because they eliminate inflammation, the vocal cords feel healthy, which creates a false confidence and tempts people to sing harder than they normally would. Good doctors will be very cautious when prescribing steroids as a solution for inflamed or swollen cords, but we should take responsibility for ourselves in that regard. I know of a singer who took steroids for six straight months because she didn't want to go to any rehearsal and not be completely "on" and impressive. She began taking steroids in an emergency situation, and it felt so good that she decided to start taking them all the time. Her voice gradually became harsh, dry, and edgy—almost plastic sounding—because the steroids obliterated any sense of vulnerability and humanity in her sound.

A NONTRADITIONAL LIFESTYLE

The life of a full-time professional singer is nontraditional at best, which is challenging for people who live in a tradition-bound world. The life of a singer is like living in New York City—people live differently here than anywhere else, at least in America. Singers are constantly on the road without the typical nine-to-five job-with-benefits kind of stability, income fluctuates constantly, and personal relationships are difficult to maintain. On the other hand, making music can be a joyful experience, and when singers are not working, their time is their own, they have a lot of flexibility in their schedules, and even though money might not come in the same amounts on a regular basis, they can make a very good living.

Some people really enjoy the itinerant life of a singer, and frankly, I think it is important to be comfortable in that lifestyle at some level to be happy doing it. All singers should think very seriously about what they need to be happy, balanced people, and if that means staying at home most of the time and consistent, regular income with benefits and a steady job, then perhaps the life of an opera singer is not a good choice. As always, the key is to know ourselves well enough to know what we need to be happy.

Some people need family and friends around them all the time, and if they are singers, they have a hard time with the itinerant lifestyle. Others manage to find friends all over the world, wherever they are singing, and that fulfills their need for companionship. I have taught many singer couples, and I know from working with them that two-singer marriages are difficult. Some of them work out, but they are always difficult, and some of the difficulty stems from disparate career paths. Inevitably, one singer's career must take precedence over the other's, or one gets a lot of work and opportunities and the other doesn't, so one of them must take a supporting role and step back from his or her own ambition to make the relationship work. That imbalance is not always fair or ideal and causes much stress.

Infidelity is another big issue for singer-couples. We are in a very passionate, emotional profession, often acting out romantic scenes on stage, connecting physically, emotionally, and artistically with colleagues, which can easily lead to romantic involvement. Also, singers on the road get lonely, so they sometimes seek to soothe that loneliness through extramarital liaisons. This can be devastating to marriages. When couples spend significant amounts of time apart, they struggle to keep their relationship balanced and growing. Many people survive by having a home base that they can always return to whenever they are not singing, and that helps create a sense of stability and consistency in their lives. But having a home base is not always possible, depending on our career goals, lifestyle, or career level.

I have no easy solution to the dilemma of living a nontraditional lifestyle, except to say that it is difficult, that we all must discover what we need personally and artistically from a singing career, and then make career choices based on those needs. For some people, family is the most important thing in their lives, and they need to have family near them all of the time, so they should make career choices that will keep them close to their families. Others have never had family or they have no desire to have a family, so they can choose to be on the road all year long. We are all different; we must find out what we need to remain balanced and then orchestrate our lives and careers to make that possible.

MENTAL HEALTH = CONFIDENCE AND HUMILITY

I do not address my students' mental health in voice lessons. Instead, I help them develop the skills and self-awareness to know their capabilities and then, by claiming those skills, the confidence to use them to their fullest capacity. Often that sense of security in singing puts them in a better place psychologically and emotionally in their personal lives. The principles of good singing apply directly to living well, and the most strikingly consistent pattern I have noticed in my students is that as they progress in their technique, they become simultaneously more confident and more humble. Confidence and humility are qualities that balance a person for singing and life.

A common personality type in this profession is the neurotic egomaniac, commonly referred to as "the jerk." The jerk constantly brags about his accomplishments, and every time you meet him you get a verbal résumé of everything he has done recently and will do in the near future, whether or not you ask for it. This is how the jerk proves to himself that he is better than everyone else. We all suffer from this tendency to some degree, and singers actually need a certain amount of bravado and confidence to be able to stand in front of thousands of people and bare our souls through singing. At the opposite extreme are those self-effacing people who are constantly putting themselves down in an attempt to gain affirmation from those around them. They drain energy from their colleagues, and people start avoiding them. For singers, it is probably better to err on the side of egomania then self-effacing, apologetic insecurity.

Confidence differs from arrogance, which overcompensates for insecurity about a perceived weakness. When we are truly confident, we simply claim what is true while humbly accepting that there are things we cannot do yet. Psychological balance is being fully in touch with reality, accepting things as they are and being open to change. Those people who either constantly tear themselves down or puff themselves up are equally out of touch with reality, and in fact, they are not so different from each other. The balanced middle between those two is to see ourselves clearly and understand both our strengths and weaknesses—claiming both and striving for flexibility and self-knowledge.

The extremes of egomania and self-deprecation are both self-centered. To be more balanced, we must learn to own our strengths and weaknesses and seek the humility to continually improve our weaknesses. I can objectively see both my students' strengths and weaknesses, so I try always to give them positive feedback, acknowledge their strengths, and then help them become receptive enough to see their weaknesses—to know where they can improve and how. As people come to fully understand their strengths, they develop confidence, and at the same time, they stay sufficiently humble to know what they cannot do and need help to develop.

Acknowledging weakness is not self-defeating if we understand that where we are is not where we always will be and change is always possible if we are open to it and seek it humbly. This kind of self-knowledge never comes to us by ourselves. We need an objective, outside source to help us see ourselves and our situation clearly and honestly. For singers, a good voice teacher can fill that role. Voice teachers provide constant, consistent feedback to help us keep a realistic perspective about our technique and performance ability. On the other hand, we should not take even our voice teachers' feedback as the gospel. We should listen to what they say; process it through our own emotional, psychological, and intellectual systems; and strive to be as honest with ourselves as we possibly can be.

> *I am not a singer that likes to be told how great I am, at least not all the time. I appreciate hearing the good, the bad and the ugly whether I want to hear it or not. It keeps me working and trying to improve.*
>
> Nicole Heaston Lane, soprano

It is amazing to me how balanced mental health comes as a by-product of learning to sing. Every singer I have taught who has fully gone through this process has become more confident and humble. That doesn't mean they are perfectly confident and humble—this is, after all, a lifelong process—but they always show progress. Like I said before, it is probably better for singers to err on the side of over-confidence. But ideally we learn to cut ourselves some slack, understanding that we are not perfect and never will be, but that change is possible and we can always improve. Singers must be confident enough to know who we are and that we have something important and significant to say. Then we need the skills and techniques to be able to share that unique message with beauty and freedom. There is an Italian phrase that says, "Come va il canto, come va la vita" (As singing goes, so goes life). That is one of the most magical aspects of learning to sing—that in singing with balance and freedom, we become more balanced and free human beings.

How to Be Successful

The typical definition of *success* is the attainment of fame and/or wealth. I believe true success is finding our own unique path and staying on it. We might become rich and famous while following that path, but fame and wealth are really only byproducts of true success, if we achieve them at all. Just as we continually examine and refine our singing, our own personal definition of success must be constantly reexamined and refined.

Singers sometimes buy into the typical definition of success and say to me, "I'll try this singing thing until I'm thirty, but if I haven't gotten to the Met by then, I'll quit." My response to those people is, "Quit now, and save all of us a lot of grief!" Any time we base our idea of success on a specific outcome, we are setting ourselves up for disappointment. If we aren't enjoying the journey, we are not likely to enjoy the destination. It is possible to debut at the Met by the age of thirty and yet not be successful. On the other hand, some people who only sing in the shower could be great successes. It all depends on your definition of *success*.

True success comes from finding and following your passion. As we uncover our naked voice to find that passion, we are successful whether or not we achieve wealth and fame. We have nothing to prove and nothing to hide. As

I indicated in the introduction, success is all about the joy we attain in *pursuit* of our passion.

I love teaching singers who are committed to continual improvement no matter where they are in their careers. For me, success in singing is all about the process of continual growth. I have seen singers in their thirties or forties who achieve a level of ability that enables them to be hired at big opera companies, and they lose their motivation for improvement. It is disturbing to see singers in the great opera houses who have quit trying to improve; therefore, they perform poorly. Because they are rich and famous (i.e., "successful" by the common definition), their poor singing is overlooked and the audiences are cheated.

To see what makes a star in the opera world, we can look at some of the "successful" singers of the past decade. They rose to fame because they showed something fresh, unique, and honest. Bryn Terfel came on the scene with his natural-sounding, big, beautiful voice and warm stage presence. Renée Fleming took the world by storm with her floating, spinning sound that was uniquely beautiful. Denyce Graves wowed people with her rich, chocolaty voice and sexy stage presence. None of these people sounded like anyone else—they all sounded like themselves. Entertainers who have enduring, long-term careers achieve fame because they seem genuine. Some nonoperatic examples include Barbra Streisand, Dolly Parton, and Patsy Cline—all of whom showed something fresh, unique, and honest.

When soprano Leontyne Price came on the scene, she forged a new path because she sang with authenticity and had the courage to be herself. Unfortunately, today when a talented African American soprano comes along, people often say, "Here comes another Leontyne Price." We are hesitant to let singers be unique; instead, we compare them with those who came before. It is uniqueness and authenticity that gets great singers noticed and launches careers. Every singer has the potential for uniqueness and authenticity.

When people start to hold onto the quality that made them special and unique in the first place, they stop improving and get stuck. This might cause them to become caricatures of their former selves. As we grow older, we become different people, and our singing should continue to grow and change as we do. I am a very different person in my fifties than I was in my twenties. I would sing anything much differently now than I would have thirty years ago, simply because my life experiences have given me new understanding and depth.

Italian soprano Mirella Freni personifies the ideal of continual growth and change over time. When she came on the scene, she was a fresh, young soubrette who sang Zerlina and Susanna with a sparkly brilliance. As she grew older, she kept changing as an artist, and she started taking on different repertoire. She was a perfect Mimi in *La Bohème*, and later in her career, singing Puccini's *Manon Lescaut*, she was still fresh and authentic. The person singing Manon Lescaut was totally different from the soubrette of her early career. As she changed as a person, she also changed and evolved as a singer and an artist, so her singing was fresh and beautiful at every stage of her career.

Anytime we imitate another singer (even if one imitates oneself), we become a caricature of a singer. This might be why people so often think of opera singers as pretentious—we often try to be something we are not. When forty-year-old singers become caricatures of their twenty-five-year-old selves, they stop developing as artists, and audiences will feel cheated, sensing something inauthentic in their performances. The path to success involves staying true to ourselves, continually trying to improve and being open to change.

When we go to the theater and we are moved by a singer's performance, it is almost always because that singer was able to strip away pretense, connect emotionally to the music, and communicate something authentic to the audience. That, to me, is a successful performance—hearing the naked voices of the singers, creating something new in each moment, connecting to that original source of utterance, and finding their own unique ways of communicating through music. As we seek to uncover the naked voice, we will always become more open, honest people. Deep within our souls, each one of us has something important to say. Successful singers are those who continually seek to free their voices so they say it clearly, honestly, and beautifully.

As I was writing this book, I solicited feedback from my current and former students. I asked them to share how the Wholistic Approach to Singing has affected their singing and their lives. It is gratifying to me to know that in teaching people to sing, I may also be helping them find their own path of *success* and authenticity. I said in the introduction that my students are the reason I wrote this book. In that spirit, I close with their own words about how their lives have changed during the process of uncovering The Naked Voice.

SASHA COOKE, MEZZO-SOPRANO

I've learned to trust my instincts both as a singer and person, which has enhanced my confidence and willingness to explore. We don't often stagnate mentally or set our mind on one thought in everyday life, so why should we do this in singing? And yet, it's so common for singers to succumb to a set of positions and tricks. Although singers think they are making it easier, they are constricting themselves. Being in the moment, re-creating the vowel, continuously touching base with the breath, and trusting our instincts are all fundamental to good singing.

Learning to sing has helped my dating life. Many women typically plan far ahead and overanalyze long afterwards. The Wholistic Approach advocates the notion of trusting and accepting where you are in your vocal development and thus in your personal life. This technique is a long and slow progression. Vocal teachers sometimes unconsciously lead a student in the direction of vocal tricks out of a desire to make them sound like an opera singer almost in a rush. Students consequently color their natural sound whether by darkening or brightening and add unnecessary tension to their technique. The Wholistic Approach predisposes people to long careers because they accept wherever they are and will be vocally. They don't try to sound like anyone other than themselves.

ALICE CONWAY, SOPRANO

I see cross-pollination in my life as a singer, attorney, and Christian. I used to oversing, argue people down, and worry as if there were no God to guide me. I strove for perfect control of every aspect of life. I have had a very hard time learning that less can be more, especially in singing. Attempting to sound like the singer I daydreamed of being, manipulating my voice, and constantly judging my sound were destructive habits that I would have continued despite their consequences. I learned not to control but to trust my voice and its supporting mechanisms and the proper technique. I learned to work with the voice I have instead of vainly trying to make it into something else. As a result, singing has become much easier, and, to my surprise, this has happened without loss of dramatic expression, although the expression sometimes feels less physically intense.

ANDREW MILLIGAN, TENOR

I think the key to my professional career as a singer, minister, and writer is built on the idea of integrity and authenticity: being honest about preparation, whether the practice room, devotional life, or research; being authentic in delivery whether producing sound, offering advice, or describing a complicated process; not being just like or sounding just like anyone other than my best self.

Teachers cannot practice for you or sing for you. What they can do is teach you how to practice, how to work, how to learn. At best they can give you a set of tools that will serve you well. We must all at one time or another leave the comfortable nest of our teacher's studio. We must become our own instructor. The best teachers understand this and prepare their students to develop their talents on their own. It's always great to come in for a tune-up, but to be truly free and authentic requires the discipline of self-discovery.

ANNETTE SONDOCK, MEZZO-SOPRANO

My singing career allows for a happy and contented personal life. I am married with a family, I hold a part-time job as a cantorial soloist at my synagogue, and travel and perform across the country and around the world. Most of my performances outside of the synagogue are by private request and for different nonprofit organizations. The techniques of the Wholistic Approach are so natural that once you understand and make use of them, producing a beautiful tone becomes as natural as breathing. Steve always told me that if I used his natural approach, I would be able to sing as long as I wanted to. I am sixty-two years old. I am singing and performing, and my voice is as rich and beautiful as it ever was.

CATHERINE HERATY, SOPRANO

The Wholistic Approach has made me more and more comfortable, allowing my voice to be what it is instead of worrying that it is inadequate and trying to fix it. It has become clear that there's nothing else I can really do but let it be what it is (and let myself be what I am) anyway!

CHRISTOPHER HERBERT, BARITONE

I think that when I am happy with myself and who I am, I sing better. I don't view my singing life and my personal life as having a clear boundary. Rather, there is a continuum. It's an interplay—when I sing well, I also feel better about myself. What I've got is what I've got. I should never be ashamed of myself, especially if I'm being true to myself and to my ambitions. I never try for more than I have, but I just tell a story about me and what I think the music says.

CLAUDIA FRIEDLANDER, SOPRANO

I believe that to achieve anything in this life, we must first form a clear, creative intention and then take dedicated action on it while remaining as detached as possible from the outcome. I also believe that our greatest potential happiness and satisfaction lies in the process of moving toward our goals rather than in the moment of their realization. If we fixate on a rigid outcome and our moment-to-moment happiness depends on how close we think we are to attaining it, it drains an incredible amount of energy and closes us off to the many unexpected twists and turns that often arise as part of the creative process. But while I do believe these things to be true and my life experience backs them up, it is still very challenging and scary to try to live this way.

In my experience, cultivating skill in this process with my singing has resulted in a greater ability to apply these principles elsewhere in life. Performances and auditions are obviously more successful and satisfying when we're completely involved in the creative process and detached from the outcome of landing a gig or pleasing an audience. Teaching is much more effective when I am able to stay with my students' immediate needs and learning patterns, rather than longing for them to achieve a certain sound or skill. Any activity, even an unpleasant one, is more effective and enjoyable when I'm able to stay focused on what I'm doing rather than worrying whether it will work, resisting the necessity of doing it, justifying my choices and methods, and all the other things that can crowd my mind and take me away from the task at hand.

DEBORAH STINSON, MEZZO-SOPRANO

The miracle of the Wholistic Approach is the simplicity of it. My life was always very complicated, and I made my singing complicated as well. The more I got into this approach, the more I changed as a person. I sometimes cried in lessons because I would not only have a vocal breakthrough but a spiritual breakthrough. I realized in these lessons that my voice was my spirit—it was uniquely mine, and so it became more beautiful the more in touch I became with my spiritual self. My voice is special to me, but I have also learned that I am much more than just a voice. I can touch lives with what I sing as long as I am true to myself and my feelings and my feelings honestly come across in my singing.

EVAN ROGISTER, BARITONE

One of the most important aspects of the Wholistic Approach is that affirmation and praise are not the means or the end goal in singing and performing. It certainly is one of the reasons we begin performing, but after a point there can never be enough praise, and performances become shallow if they are all about "Please love me." Instead, singing has to bring you joy, excitement, a sensual release—any number of personal satisfactions. Otherwise the artist is not growing naturally, but how he percieves people would want him to grow. This is the "path"—the route that an artist must take in order to be true to himself and his talent. The path is often not accompanied by immediate success or fame, and one has to accept that these may never come. And it often requires sticking to your own artistic principals when no one else is recognizing or supporting your talent.

Both the Inventions and the concept of the path all stem from the idea that singing is one of the most honest and vulnerable acts a human can engage in. If the singer is not honest with himself and about his own gifts and limitations, then he will not be true to the music and his fakery will be instantly recognizable to others. What instantly attracts us to great artists is their honesty and the Wholistic Approach is all about training true artists.

HOLLY BEWLAY, SOPRANO

It was so hard for me to enjoy singing once singing became an occupation. The Wholistic Approach helped me understand how to enjoy the process (the way to get to the destination) rather than the result—to "enjoy the ride." I enjoy every day's progress more now.

GRETCHEN FARRAR, SOPRANO

Focusing on intention is a wonderful goal, and I constantly aspire to intend positively as a singer and in life. Part of the challenge is having a concept of what one is intending. And intention goes for life as well. If I walk around thinking "don't be negative," I'll stay negative. Positive intention is so much more freeing. It may be initially challenging, especially if it's not one's normal thought pattern, but committing to the process feels better anyway.

JEFF MONETTE, BARITONE

You can't sing your best if you are not happy. I also think that your true voice is literally who you truly are. There is no difference in finding your voice and finding who you are as a person—they are the same journey. So many times, we try to put vocal "Band-Aids" on or try to sing the way we think we should or how we think someone wants us to. The Wholistic Approach is all about the process, which in turn frees you to have a more authentic product.

I have always thought of myself as an underdog vocally. I never had an amazing voice. It was always good enough for where I was, but not for where I wanted to be. I had to accept that I could sound different and embrace change. I am just working on the best me I can be and not trying to mold it into something, which has helped my tendency to judge my voice. Taking away all of the effort and becoming so naked vocally takes courage.

I have learned that my biggest problems in my singing coincide with my greatest issues with myself on a personal level. I need to remember that I don't have to be so careful in my singing. I always want to be the good student and get everything right. But what I have learned is that in singing, the more you try to control the voice, the less it works. I am learning to trust my voice and trust myself. I haven't become reckless by any means, but I have learned to let go and let whatever comes out be all right. There has been a change in my life as well, as I have learned that I don't need to be so careful and I don't need to control everything. I have to trust. I mostly have to trust my body to know what the voice needs, and I don't need to work so hard. In fact, the harder I work, the more I work against the nature of the voice. As Steve says, you need to be somewhat kamikaze about singing. You need to take a leap of faith and accept what comes out. It's an extremely fulfilling approach to both singing and to life.

Jonathan Knapp, Tenor

I find music and performing to be an integral part of my life, and as such, the more I perform and express myself through music, the better I feel about myself. The exciting thing about learning to be a better technical singer is that a good technique allows you to concentrate more of your energies on the characterization and the performance rather than focusing on or worrying about the instrument. I recall watching Joyce DiDonato and Daniel Belcher [two students of Steve Smith], performing in *La Cenerentola,* and the most impressive element of their techniques was not the freedom in their tone, the breadth of their range, or even the facility of their coloratura, which was remarkable. What left the strongest impression was how their technique was so ingrained and automatic that they were completely free in their body to be engaging to the audience and perfectly natural on stage.

Joyce DiDonato, Mezzo-Soprano

Like most activities that require total excellence, what you learn in your lessons and experiences can often apply to everyday life. There have been a number of anecdotes that I have carried away from a lesson, only to realize it held a lot of truth in everyday life. My favorite came during my second year of studying with Steve Smith. I was at the critical point of learning to trust all that I had begun to understand; however, I was still deathly afraid of slipping back into old habits, such as cracking wildly on any note in my upper passaggio! Steve identified in one critical lesson that I was holding my breath to avoid cracking rather than moving the breath steadily on a pure vowel, which of course, if employed correctly would never result in a cracked note. He simply said, "Joyce, never avoid doing the negative . . . always *do* the positive." This is something that has crossed over into many facets of my thinking, and I've realized it is such a powerful way to approach life: It puts you in control of accomplishing what you intend to achieve.

KEN BRYSON, TENOR

One of my greatest challenges as a singer both technically and personally was to allow myself to let go. I like to be in control of all aspects of my life, especially in my singing. Through the Wholistic Approach, I gradually began to gain the freedom I needed to loosen the grips I had placed on myself both technically and personally as a singer. It is still very much an ongoing process to rid myself of these controls, but it is certainly something I do not believe I would have been able to reach without learning to sing. In applying the Wholistic Approach, you must give yourself completely over to the process. The reason, as with anything you do in life, is if you do not commit yourself fully to this process, you will not reach its full benefits. The approach is simple; it teaches the student the basic building blocks, which guarantee a strong and healthy voice for the future.

KIMAKO TROTMAN, BASS

There is purpose in your passion to sing. Trust that you are in the right place and that there is a natural connection between you and your goal. First, calm down your world to see if your goal is really yours and not your environment's goal for you. Then, learn to develop your intuition (heart) to bring you to the right relationships and wisdom. As you go further with courage, you'll never fail.

LEAH TSAMOUS, MEZZO-SOPRANO

Being a singer *was* my personal life. Everything I was doing was inexorably linked to my singing. How I felt about myself as a singer defined how I felt about myself as a person. Naturally, getting a grasp on my voice and getting a technique that allowed me to be consistent really helped my self-esteem. Even if I wasn't "really good," I knew I wouldn't be "really bad." Before, I could never count on how anything would come out of my mouth. The connection between my voice and my life led to either highs or lows in my singing and therefore highs or lows in my life. Learning a consistent technique helped me have consistency in my life, and consistency in my life led to consistency in my singing. Being on an even keel is much easier than being manic.

MARTI NEWLAND, SOPRANO

Vocal pedagogy, as a whole, embraces language entailing, "don't," "shouldn't," "can't," and "won't." In drastic contrast is the Wholistic Approach, which remains positive at all times. This has empowered me with self-compassion in vocal development. This positive attitude extends into all aspects of my life, reminding me that there is always a positive approach.

MATTHEW MORRIS, TENOR

The effects of my voice lessons continue throughout the week. Simply put, learning that singing is not impossible and that the actual learning process of singing can be clear, precise and fun, allowed me to lose a few of my neuroses. The change has definitely been one from the inside out. I did not actively seek to change myself, my habits, my surroundings, and so on, but rather the new-found confidence gained from my lessons has allowed me to be a person that I've always wanted to be. My friends say that I am so much more dependable and emotionally available than ever before. My parents remark how they finally see me as a young adult and no longer just a child. I personally realize that I am happier for a longer period of time than I have ever been in my life.

RICARDO LUGO, BASS

It takes time and patience to understand the Inventions; but once you have them, your work will be very easy. Now I am able to go to any coach, conductor, or other voice teacher and be capable of understanding what they are asking me for—this can happen without any possible chance of ruining my voice or my technique.

ROLANDO SANZ, TENOR

I have always sought a balance between my singing career and my personal life. Once I began pursuing this career, I promised myself that I would never compromise myself or my loved ones for my career. As a result, I truly consider myself a stronger performer who is pursuing this career on my terms. The support of my loved ones has allowed me to keep my head on straight and treat this seemingly roller-coaster business as just another day at the office. As performers, we are generally highly emotional people. But as a result of having a wonderful home life, I am able to separate myself from my art and not allow successes and failures to affect me so emotionally that I question who I am as a person or as a performer.

SUNYOUNG KIM, SOPRANO

Like total isolation of muscles gives strength in singing; total independence gives maturity in singing and life. Otherwise, one may need a teacher in every difficult or important situation, such as big performance or audition. In reality, since the teacher cannot always be there, one may lack confidence or stability. Dependency would keep me immature in singing and life as well.

TIFFANY JACKSON, SOPRANO

My singing career and personal life are one and the same. Singing is my life and the closest people to me understand that. Ultimately, singing is not something I chose; it chose me. It is a means to my mission (whatever that is!). There are times when my life conflicts with the singing because there are sacrifices you must make if you sing. It is not a "normal" existence because, unlike a piano or a violin, the instrument itself is within the body. Whatever is going on inside and outside the body, the voice is affected. Ultimately, it's all about balance. Natural ability is just that, natural. Natural is like a child. Learning to sing is about stripping away the baggage that life brought in order to uncover the natural. It can take a lifetime, but only the strong survive.

WALDO GONZALEZ, TENOR

Violinists pack up their instrument, physically remove it from their shoulder, and put it in a case for the night. Our instrument never leaves. As artists, we all have the privilege of being emotionally connected to our craft and instrument, but it cannot be understated that singers are physically connected to their instrument as well. For any musician, your personal life plays a significant role in your art, but finding the release in the fact that we're making music for our supper and not sitting in a cubicle behind a computer screen ten hours per day is the challenge.

The hardest thing to understand when you've had success is why you need to change to get better. I spent two whole years unlearning detrimental muscle memory and bad habits in the interest of totally stripping my voice to its core (talking and breath), and using that breath to energize the talking. I then spent two years building my voice into an instrument that could at least be "worked on." At that point, I could audibly improve. You have to believe, and you must trust your teacher. When you do that, time becomes an ally in your pursuit of understanding that which puzzles you.

Michael Slattery, Tenor

By letting go, and by accepting the unique qualities of one's pure voice, the singer succeeds in getting back to what is true. From that place, the text one is singing begins to ring true. The Wholistic Approach encourages that beautiful surrender that we artists are eternally re-creating on our journey to truth in expression.

Heidi Moss Sali, Soprano

For me, learning to sing was not just a vocal change but a life change. I was able to switch careers—from scientist to musician—and actually pursue singing as a profession. Now, I am an active musician in San Francisco, a far cry from the lab bench.

However, it goes beyond that. I always make the joke about the book *All I Really Need to Know I Learned in Kindergarten*. I think the same can be said for the Wholistic Approach. The combination of elegant simplicity, calm observation of the present, and allowing the natural sound to take over is a model for life. It has made me a better person for sure. We need to strip things down to their bare essentials, observe not force, and allow beauty to be, not judge the past or anxiously predict the future. It is about the present moment and freedom. I realize it's corny, but alas, it is true.

And we have to work every day to do that. It is a never-ending process, and I will never stop using these tools to improve.

Robert Chionis, Baritone

I discovered that I wasn't the type of person to lead an emotionally turbulent life and retain the poise that was necessary for me to sing well. This has informed many of my personal life decisions as well as career decisions I have made, specifically job offers that I have turned down or contracts that I have chosen not to extend. Somewhere along the way, I realized that it was much more important to me to be honest as a singing performer and to sing as well as I can than it was to have a "great" career.

I have found that there is an interesting correlation between singing with less entanglement and finding greater satisfaction in my personal life. By seeking to strip away the resistance to my breath flow and give up holding onto my voice, I move toward a more genuine way of singing. Even though this way of singing is more authentic, it makes me feel vulnerable and exposed. It requires me to have trust and faith in the end result. Likewise, in my personal life, when I let go of my desire to defend myself or control what is happening, I am much more "in the moment" and able to have a true and honest experience. Although it is difficult to allow myself to let my guard down and go with the flow, I ultimately gain a deeper connection to the world around me. In singing or in life in general, staying open and present allows for the greatest rewards. The real challenge to achieving those rewards is letting go of the fears and insecurities that plague all of us. It is easier said than done, but it's possible to experience this freedom of voice or mind with an open perspective and dedicated practice.

Audio Samples on CD

1. Comparison of Vernacular and Refined Speech
   Singer 1
2. Simple, Natural, Vernacular Speaking
   Singers 2, 3, 4, 5
3. Speaking with Projection
   Singers 2, 3, 4, 5
4. Speaking with Line
   Singers 2, 3, 4, 5
5. Speaking with Projection and Line on Pitch
   Singers 2, 3, 4, 5, 6, 7, 8, 9, 10, 11, 12, 13
6. The Downward Sigh
   Singers 7, 4, 1, 12
7. The Siren
   Singers 14, 8, 15, 1, 13, 12
8. The Sigh with Descending Five-Tone Scale
   Singers 2, 14, 7, 4, 16, 6, 8, 3, 17, 10, 1, 13, 5, 12
9. The Arpeggio
   Singers 8, 6, 2, 10, 3, 5, 13

10. Detached [ɑ]'s
    Singers 16, 6, 14, 7, 2, 10, 5, 1, 13
11. [ɑ] Sung Correctly and Incorrectly
    Singer 1
12. Detached [ɑ]'s and Forced Glottal Closure [ɑ]'s
    Singer 1
13. The Wobble
    Singers 6, 8, 2, 10, 1, 13
14. The Eleven-Tone scale
    Singers 16, 14, 10, 13, 3
15. (Singing "The Love of Fudge") Converting Accented [ʌ]
    and Unaccented [ə] to [ɑ]
    Singer 1
16. (Singing "Drat that Cat") Keeping [æ] Vertical
    Singer 1
17. French Nasal Vowels
    Singer 1
18. Double Consonants
    Singer 1
19. Consonant Substitutions
    Singer 1
20. Crescendo and Decrescendo
    Singer 1
21. Divide into Pulses
    Singer 5
22. Sing the Pulses Legato
    Singer 5
23. Sing All the Notes Pulse by Pulse
    Singer 5
24. Combine Two Pulses at a Time
    Singer 5
25. Combine All Pulses
    Singer 5
26. Five-Step Process on Rossini
    Singer 18
27. Supraglottal Aspiration in *Fioratura*
    Singer 19
28. Staccato/Legato [ɑ]'s
    Singer 1

29. Staccato Passage from Queen of the Night's Aria from Mozart's
     The Magic Flute
          Singer 15
30. Speaking the Text in Monotone
          Singer 1
31. Phrase-by-Phrase Translation
          Singer 1
32. Speaking the Text as a Dramatic Reading
          Singer 1

Performer Credits for Audio Samples

SINGERS

(1) W. Stephen Smith

(2) Amy Buckley

(3) Aaron Blake

(4) Marti Newland

(5) Weston Hurt

(6) Christina Carr

(7) Kathryn Skemp

(8) Sasha Cooke

(9) Claudia Friedlander

(10) David Salsbery Fry

(11) Tobey D. Miller

(12) Brian Mulligan

(13) Scott Murphree

(14) Anne Jennifer Nash

(15) Julie Liston Johnson

(16) Stephanie E. Tennill

(17) Evan Rogister
(18) Ross Chitwood
(19) Joyce DiDonato

PIANIST

Carol Mannen Smith

Index

[ɑ] vowel, 59
  [ɑ]-family vowel exercise, 60
  ideal vowel to achieve balance, 60
  magically centered, 59
  Midwestern pronunciation of, 60
  specific use of, 59
  abduction, 16
accompaniment, 142
acting in opera, 144, 145
adduction, 16, 17
adductor muscles, 63, 71, 95, 96, 119, 167
aerobic exercise, 168
agility, 118, 119
airflow, 48
  carrying the sound, 69
  responsive to speaking, 89
air pressure, 39, 40
air waves, 16
Alexander Technique, 37
Allen, Ferris, 25
amplification, 125, 126
antibiotics, 19, 20, 21

antihistamines, 165
anti-legato, 115
Ariadne auf Naxos (Strauss), 168
Armistead, Christine, 52, 139
arpeggio, the, 81, 82, 83
arrogance, 176
articulators, 57
  independent function of, 57, 62, 89
  keeping consistent, 76
Aspen Music Festival and School, 8,
    39
aspiration, supraglottal, 122
attack, 85, 86, 91
attire, in rehearsal, 159
audiation, 142
audition repertoire, 131–132
  industry standard for, 131
auditions, 137–140
  apologetic, 138
  as performances, 140
  pet peeves in, 138–139
  successful, 137

199

authenticity, 3, 181
  pursuit of, 4
automatic transmission, 99

Bach, J. S., 9
back space, 47, 72
  beautiful sound through, 47, 72
  blooming in, 78
  key to accessing top range, 72
baggage, 135, 140
balance, struggle to find, 79
balanced sound, 46, 81
  heard over an orchestra, 81
  sensation of, shifting through range,
    98
Balancing Act, A (The Third Invention),
    46, 79–83, 139
bariatric surgery, 169
  change in sensation as a result
    of, 170
  increased localized effort from, 170
  a serious issue, 169
baritones, 55
base of the tongue, 63
  no movement in, during onset, 92
  tension in, 63–64
bass voices, 55
beeper analogy, 52
belting, 100, 126–127
  easier for smaller voices, 127
Bernoulli Effect, the, 16–17
Bewlay, Holly, 185
Bible, the, 6, 37
"blatty" speech, 51
body alignment, 37–38
  necessary for free-flowing breath, 37
body fat, advantage from when exhaling,
    169–170
brain, left side of, 23–24
brain, true generator for voice, 52
breath, 33
  deep, for singing, 37
  essence of life, 34
  nourishes the voice, 42
  preparatory, 34
  source of life, 33

breath flow, consistent, 74
breathing, 13, 33–42
  approaches to, 34–35
  bad habits in, 35
  first life-giving activity, 13
  involuntary activity, 34
  in natural childbirth, 33
  for speech, 52
breath pressure, 67–68
breath support, 39
  doing sit-ups to enhance, 40
Brewer, Christine, 39
Britten, Benjamin, operas of, 115
Broadway singing, 86, 100, 125–127
Brothers, Richard, 7
Bryson, Ken, 187
busy singers, 157

Callas, Maria, 135
calories, 164, 167
Cancun, 24
caricatures, 180
Carmen (Bizet), 133–135
cartilages
  arytenoid, 69, 71
  rocking motion of, 95
  thyroid, 69
categorization of voices, 125, 132
  subjective nature of, 132
change, being open to, 176, 181
Chatauqua Opera, 146
chest cavity, 16
  expansion of, in breathing, 35–37
  as secondary resonator, 16
chest voice, 99–100
  carrying high in belt method, 126
  female fear of using, 100
chiaro, 45–46, 67, 80–81, 89, 98
  terms that evoke, 46
chiaroscuro, 45–47, 81, 83
  definition of, 45–46
  ratio shifting through range, 82
Chionis, Robert, 190
chipmunk teeth technique, 114
choosing repertoire, 130–136, 151–152
Church of Christ, 5

classical technique, 81
    foundation for any genre, 81
clean signal, 50, 80
Cline, Patsy, 180
clothing, 4
    stripping away layers of, 25
colleague, being a good, 157–158
coloratura sopranos, 55
coloring the sound, 145
concert music, 154–156
conditioning the voice, 107
conductors, dealing with, 154–156
confidence and humility, 139, 176
congestion, 16, 165
consequences, 148, 153
consonant clusters, 114
consonants, 51, 112
    articulating, 112
    double and single, 112
    "spitting out," 112
context, singing difficult passages
        in, 90
contraltos, 55, 77
control, letting go of, 23, 42, 69, 86, 93, 96
    in larynx, 93
    power through, 69
    true freedom through, 91
conventional medicine, 20
Conway, Alice, 182
Cooke, Sasha, 88, 181
core, 32, 46, 50
country music singers, 125
Covent Garden, 168
covering the vowel, 109
cracking the voice, 65
creativity, 26
crescendo, 116, 118, 194
crying, 27–28
cut, through orchestra, 81
    naturally occurring, 81
cutoff, 91

Daniels, Annette, 146
decrescendo, 92, 116, 118, 194
defined vowels, 48
descending five-tone scale, 75–78

Des Moines Metro Opera, 8, 146
detached vowel onset, 86–91
diaphragm, 15, 35
    action of, in breathing, 35
    location of, 35
    shape of, 35
diction, 115
    detrimental to good singing, 115
    means to an end, 115
    purpose of good, 115
DiDonato, Joyce, 63–64, 80, 186–187
diet and exercise, 167–168
diphthong, 56–57, 58, 59
directing airflow, 73
directors, 154–156
discipline, 150, 153, 165, 168
dividing music into pulses, 119–122
Don Giovanni (Mozart), 134
    women's roles in, 134
Don Pasquale (Donizetti), 136
double consonants, 112–113
    tendency to increase pressure, 113
downward pressure, 60, 77, 125
downward sigh, the, 70–71, 193
downward space, 47, 72
"drainful" people, 158
dramatic mezzo-sopranos, 55, 134
dramatic sopranos, 55, 130, 133,
        134, 144
drawl, eliminating, 31
drugs, 19
dynamics, 116–118

[e] vowel, 58
    problematic for English speakers, 58
    rolling effect of tongue to produce, 58
educational institutions, 153
egomania, erring on the side of, 176
egomaniacs, 176
Elektra (Strauss), 144
eleven-tone scale, 98, 100
emotional intent of music, 115
environment, musical, 142
environmental influences, eliminating,
        50
evaluation, 23–24

magical [ɑ] vowel, 88
    must be mentally defined, 88
Magic Flute, The (Mozart), 91, 123
male voice, 55
    high range of, 73
    speaking range, 55
malnourishing the voice, 41
manipulating the voice, 99
Mannen, Carol, 7
Manon Lescaut (Puccini), 181
manual transmission, 99
manufacturing shift in voice, 99
margin of error, 88, 173
marketing, 130, 136
marking, 143, 144, 159, 173
masseter muscle, 110, 164
    remains relaxed in singing, 110
mechanical objects, 17, 18
meditation, 137
memorization, 148
mental health, 176, 177
messa di voce, 103
Messiah (Handel), 119
middle range of voice, 56
Mignon (Thomas), 134, 135
Milligan, Andrew, 35, 182
miracles, 10
mistakes, learning from, 25
mixing head and chest voice, 99
moderation, learning, 80
modulation of vocal function, 97, 98, 99
Monette, Jeff, 185
Morris, Matthew, 188
motion, constant, 23, 26
motivation, 9, 180
mouth, as resonator, 16
    changing shape of, 16
Mozart, Wolfgang Amadeus, 124
    holding back the voice to sing, 124
    music good for all voice types, 124
Mozart voices, 125
mucus, crucial lubricant of voice, 166
Murphree, Scott, 191
musical art, 26
musicality, 116–117

musical sounds, ingredients of, 14–17
    in various instruments, 14–16
musical theater singing, 125, 126

naked, 3–4
nasal cavities, 14, 15, 16
National Association of Teachers of
    Singing (NATS), 39
neurological impulse to speak, 54, 85
neurotic people, 158, 176
Newland, Marti, 188
Newton's third law of motion, 41
nodules, 171–173
    treatable without surgery, 171
    vocal exercises used to treat, 171
nonclassical styles, 125
"Non più mesta," 64
nontraditional lifestyle, 174
Norma (Bellini), 159

[o] vowel, 60
    opens up resonators, 71–72
    refining, 60
O'Hara, Scarlet, 134
Oklahoma Christian College, 7
Oklahoma City University, 7
onset, 85
    glottal, 86
    lack of entanglement in, 92
Opera in the Ozarks, 8
origin, of book, 9
oscuro, 47, 89, 97–98
    airflow a key to, 72
    terms that evoke, 47
overadducted folds, 67, 167
over-confidence, 177

pacing oneself, 150
Pagliacci (Leoncavallo), 136
parachute analogy, 72
Paris, disappointing trip to, 24
park-and-bark, 145
Parton, Dolly, 180
parts, examining in relationship to
    whole, 28

success, definitions of, 179
  by-products of, 179
support, 39–40
supraglottal entanglement, 52, 89
supraglottal pressure, 50
surge of air, 95
Susannah (Floyd), 134
S-word, the, 39

taking responsibility, 151
Tannhäuser (Wagner), 133
tape, sound of voice on, 29
Tebaldi, Renata, 134
technical ability, maturation of, 135
technique, 21–24
  definition of, 21
  Stradivarius analogy regarding, 21–22
television, effect on opera, 168
tenors, 55
tension, eliminating unnecessary, 37
Terfel, Bryn, 180
thoracic cavity, 41
time, necessary for progress, 75
time management, 148
Tines, Laca, 83
tone of voice, 29
tones, manufactured, 22
tongue, arch of, 57, 58
tongue muscle, 63
tongue position, 57
tongue tension, 63
tongue vowels, 62
Tosca (Puccini), 134
touch action of glottis, 90
trachea, 16, 35, 63
training the voice, 107
tricks, 20, 181
trip, take the, 24
Trotman, Kimako, 187
trouser roles, 155
true, being, to oneself, 129
truth, veiling the, 49
Tsamous, Leah, 187
turning down offers, 149
  reasons for, 156

two-singer marriages, 175

[u] vowel, 60
  different from everyday speech, 61
  lip movement needed to form, 60
  refining, 60
ulterior motives, 49
unhealthy vocal habits, 165
unhinging the jaw, 110
University of Houston, 8
upward space, 47
urine, color of, 165

Verdi, Giusseppe, 125
Verdi voices, 125
vernacular speech, 30–32, 50
  as beginning point, 31
vibrator, 14
visual art, nature of, 23
visual realism, expectation of, 168
vocal art, nature of, 23
  difference from visual art, 23
vocal coaches, 132, 158
vocal cords, 16
  staying flabby and loose, 73, 96
  stretch long for high pitches, 70
vocal folds, 15
  differences in, 15
  minimal engagement of, 67
vocalis muscle, 67
  eliminating vibration of, 70
vocal mechanism, the, 68
vocal problems, addressing at root, 20–21
vocally uncomfortable music, 132
voice, 82
  keeping relaxed, 82
  medium of communication, 145
voice teachers, role of, 177
Voigt, Deborah, 168
  bariatric surgery of, 169
  little black dress incident, 169
volume of air, changes in, 42
vowel definition, 83, 108
  freedom through, 108
  in singing, different than speech, 109